theatre practice and another about solo performers.

Cairney's paintings have been exhibited in New Zealand and in Scotland. His *Nine Lives of Burns* were shown at the Burns Birthplace Museum, Alloway in 2012 and more recently his *Stations of the Cross* were displayed in Glasgow as part of the Lentfest Festival 2014 and at St Bride's Church in Bothwell. His most recent project, a series of paintings called *The Marian Way*, was exhibited in St Patrick's Church, Glasgow during October 2015. John still finds time for solo appearances and book shows.

By the same author:

Miscellaneous Verses
A Moment White
The Man Who Played Robert Burns
East End to West End
Worlds Apart
A Year Out in New Zealand
A Scottish Football Hall of Fame
On the Trail of Robert Burns
Solo Performers
The Quest for Robert Louis Stevenson
The Quest for Charles Rennie Mackintosh
Heroes Are Forever
Glasgow By the Way, But
Flashback Forward
Greasepaint Monkey
The Sevenpenny Gate
Burnscripts
The Importance of Being

The Tycoon and the Bard

The Tycoon and The Bard

Andrew Carnegie and Robert Burns

How the world's richest man was inspired by Scotland's greatest poet

John Cairney

Luath Press Limited
EDINBURGH
www.luath.co.uk

First Published 2016

ISBN: 978-1-910021-96-5

The paper used in this book is recyclable. It is made
from low chlorine pulps produced in a low energy,
low emissions manner from renewable forests.

Images of Burns and the Burns Cottage sourced
from Wikimedia where they have been identified
as being in the public domain.

Photographic images of Andrew Carnegie's life
courtesy of Andrew Carnegie Birthplace Museum.

Designed and typeset by Mark Hosker

Printed and bound by
The Charlesworth Group, Wakefield

Contents

Acknowledgements

I must first thank my daughter Jane Livingstone, a writer herself, whose idea it was that the lecture I gave on Carnegie's admiration of Robert Burns at the Andrew Carnegie Birthplace Museum in 2011 might be the basis for a slim volume.

The initial project was encouraged by Angus Hogg, Chairman of the Dunfermline Burns Club and facilitated by Chief Executive of the Carnegie Dunfermline Trust, Nora Rundell, who gave approval for me to approach Lorna Owers, Curator at the Birthplace Museum, to undertake the appropriate preliminary research. My research also included contact with the Greenock Burns Club and the Robert Burns World Federation at Kilmarnock.

This was the ring of support created for the text to be written and submitted to Gavin MacDougall at Luath Press who commissioned a book with cover and illustrations by Mark Hosker of 13hundred Creative Partners in Edinburgh. I am also indebted to Katharine Liston for her scrutiny of the text. I sincerely thank all of the above for making this book possible.

Preface

It's a well-known fact that Andrew Carnegie, the Dunfermline-born industrialist, was a passionate admirer of the poet Robert Burns. This throws an interesting new light on the character and reputation of Carnegie. That he was inspired from youth and throughout his life by a poet – and an egalitarian, intensely romantic one at that – is perhaps at odds with Carnegie's image as a ruthless capitalist. Nor was his admiration for Burns some hobbyist whim. There is clear evidence that Carnegie put both his actions and his money where his passion was. Not only did he stipulate that a bust – not of himself but of Burns, Scotland's national poet – be installed in each of the 2,811 free libraries he famously gifted around the world, but two papers held in the Andrew Carnegie Birthplace Museum in Dunfermline demonstrate the exact nature of his regard. The first is the address Carnegie delivered in 1912 at the unveiling of a statue of Burns in Montrose. Carnegie had contributed to the funding of the statue at a time when other benefactors had been hard to find and in his speech he extols Burns' virtues at length and with great conviction. The second paper is 'Genius Illustrated from Burns', an essay in which Carnegie captures the essence of Burns' prodigious talent. These papers are quoted throughout this volume.

'Genius' was the mystery in Burns that first attracted Carnegie: 'Talent has climbed Parnassus... Genius alone has scaled heights and revealed to us the enchanted land beyond and over the mountain-top.' However, Carnegie revered Burns not only as a poet but as a philosopher and a prophet. He saw him as a challenger of religious dogma and a champion of republican democracy. Carnegie shared Burns' love of laughter and song and was also deeply touched by the poet's tender humanity, his respect for all living things and compassion for human frailty: 'his spontaneous, tender, all-pervading sympathy with every form of misfortune, pain or grief; not only in man but in every created form of being. He loved all living things, both great and small.' As a writer himself, Carnegie greatly appreciated too Burns' vivid leaps of imagination and immaculate word choice.

Born in humble circumstances – Burns almost 80 years before Carnegie – both men had, by their mid-30s, already achieved on a colossal scale. Burns was to die at only 37, leaving behind a body of work of such quality that it would ensure his lasting legacy. Andrew Carnegie had by the age of 33 pledged in a memo to himself to give away any surplus income beyond $50,000 a year, for the good of his fellow man. In so doing he, in effect, became the father of modern philanthropy. How truly remarkable that two young men from the same small country should entertain such powerful instincts which would do so much to shape the world.

Burns is loved the world over but, while he is recognised for his success and good deeds to this day, there are those who judge Andrew Carnegie harshly for his record as an employer, particularly on account of the incident at Homestead Steel Works (of which more later). Carnegie was however a typical employer of his day and, while Homestead did indeed damage his reputation, there is yet much to admire. He directed much of his philanthropy toward the education of workers (including women – Carnegie believed he owed everything good in life to his mother and his wife), as well as gifting libraries and technical institutes musical instruments and countless other benefactions. He took a passionate stance against slavery and war and was, unusually for the time, strongly opposed to racism, contributing to the funding of Tuskegee College for Colored Teachers and providing a pension for its founder, Booker T Washington. He believed the rich should be taxed more severely than the poor and that every citizen should have a vote. He introduced pensions for his workers, and for many teachers, and set up trusts for the effective and continuing disbursement of his fortune after his death. One of the trusts most precious to him was the Hero Fund for the recognition of those who lost their lives in acts of peacetime heroism.

In a life that was much honoured, Carnegie never hid his delight in being made an Honorary Vice-President of the Burns Federation and took great pride in being elected a life member of the Greenock Burns Club, the oldest Burns Club in the world: fitting tributes to his practical efforts to make Burns better known around the globe, especially in the United States.

Andrew Carnegie drew on the poetry and ideas of 'his favourite' Burns for both inspiration and solace: this modest book attempts to show how this, combined with a shared belief in the 'brotherhood of man', underpins the respect that one famous Scot felt for another, a respect that was to be both life-changing and lifelong.

John Cairney
Glasgow, 2016

The Tycoon and The Bard

Andrew Carnegie and Robert Burns

Humble Beginnings

ANDREW CARNEGIE, the first son in a poor weaver's family, was born in Dunfermline, Fife, during a thunderstorm on the night of 25 November 1835. Similarly, Burns was born in a storm in Ayrshire as a poor farmer's son on the night of 25 January 1759.

Each was his own man, distinctive and individual, but the common thread was their deep passion for equality in all humanity. This showed itself in almost every line of Burns' poetry and in many of his songs.

Carnegie called Burns the 'Apostle of Democracy' and frequently upheld the poet's egalitarian vision. This twinning of views may go some way towards understanding the bond that tied an industrial giant, who became a multi-billionaire, to a literary genius who died in comparative poverty. Carnegie was unashamedly fired by the genius of Burns from early boyhood and he was never to lose this unbridled enthusiasm for the man or his work. Naturally, this relationship was one-sided. Burns died 39 years before Carnegie was born but the farmer-poet had written words that inspired Carnegie to a genuine devotion that was to last until his own death in 1919.

Burns and Carnegie, born 76 years apart on opposite coasts of the same land, shared a hunger for knowledge. They pounced on that same God-given thread and used it to create their own individual coat. They read everything and anything that came to hand, training their memories to store information – an ability that was later to stand both in good stead.

Burns was taught first by his father and then, although poor, by a hired tutor, John Murdoch, who had him reading, at the age of seven, the New Testament, Fisher's *English Grammar*, the *Spelling Book* and Masson's Collection of Prose and Verse. For relief there was *The Life of Hannibal* and the *History of William Wallace*. Carnegie, on the other hand, equally poor, read only what was available from his father and relatives, friends and neighbours. In this way, at only ten, he discovered Robert Burns and was never to let him go. It was a relationship that offered inspiration and practical sustenance, especially towards the end of his life.

Burns, arguably the world's most famous Scotsman, was voted Scot of the Millennium by the Scottish people in 2000. There are clubs devoted to him in 200 countries and there are more statues of him around the world than of any other literary or cultural figure. The first stone was raised to him in Bombay in 1812. This need for a sculpted image is perhaps understood when one remembers that the Victorian Age that followed Burns was the age of statues, just as in the later epoch of Carnegie, a man's status was judged by how big an estate he left, although Carnegie himself held the view that 'the man who dies thus rich dies disgraced'. Carnegie is for all his deeds for the common good, his humanitarian values and his much publicised vast wealth is, by comparison with Burns, almost anonymous to today's generation.

Andrew, age 16, with younger brother Tom ▶

Carnegie's knowledge of the work of Burns started early in life in Rolland Street, Dunfermline, just down the hill from the Carnegies' home in Moodie Street. A Mr Robert Martin ran his Lancastrian School, a form of peer-taught school popular at that time, for a penny per week per child and Andrew started there when he was eight. Schooling was not compulsory in 1843 and it was less the cost that deterred many weaving families from enrolling their children as the loss of a much-needed pair of hands. The Carnegies told Andrew they would not send him to school unless he asked to go. Carnegie chose to go and was added to the already large class controlled by Dominie Martin and his team of unqualified pupil-teachers. With such numbers in one large room, discipline had to be strict, but young Andrew was an eager pupil and before long he was known to all as 'Snuffy Martin's pet'. It was not a title the boy relished.

Significantly, it was in learning a Burns poem that Carnegie first showed his skill as a memoriser, and what is more relevant, bearing in mind his future money-making propensities, he was paid for it. For the princely sum of one penny, exactly the amount paid each week for his schooling, he recited Burns' 'Man Was Made to Mourn'. It was a mammoth undertaking and an amazing feat of memory for a boy of his age.

There are 11 verses in it and every one of them must have hung heavily over the heads of the children in that cold, crowded Victorian classroom on that winter's day as young Carnegie went in front of his classmates to read:

When chill November's surly blast
Made fields and forests bare,
One ev'ning, as I wander'd forth,
Along the banks of Ayr,
I spy'd a man, whose aged step
Seem'd weary, worn with care;
His face was furrow'd o'er with years,
And hoary was his hair.

'Young stranger, whither wand'rest thou?'
Began the rev'rend Sage;
'Does thirst of wealth thy step constrain,
Or youthful Pleasure's rage?
Or haply, prest with cares and woes,
Too soon thou hast began,
To wander forth, with me, to mourn
The miseries of Man.
...

Look not alone on youthful Prime,
Or Manhood's active might;
Man then is useful to his kind,
Supported in his right:
But see him on the edge of life,
With Cares and Sorrows worn,
Then Age and Want, Oh! ill-match'd pair!
Show Man was made to mourn.

'Ill-matched' Burns and Carnegie certainly were not, despite their physical contrast – Burns dark-eyed, Carnegie fair-haired. Like Burns, Carnegie had an alert mind and a tremendous admiration for the word, written or spoken. The young Carnegie read in Burns how some are born lucky, but most are not and these words would have reflected the social beliefs already instilled by his own family:

> *A few seem favourites of Fate,*
> *In Pleasure's lap caress'd;*
> *Yet, think not all the Rich and Great,*
> *Are likewise truly blest.*
> *But Oh! what crowds in ev'ry land,*
> *All wretched and forlorn,*
> *Thro' weary life this lesson learn,*
> *That Man was made to mourn.*

In 1784 Burns had told his brother, Gilbert, on their Mossgiel Farm, that he could not conceive a more mortifying picture of human life than a man seeking work. How did he know this? He had never tested the work market, having been in thrall to the family farm since he could walk. It is remarkable that here was a young man in his early 20s, living on a farm in a remote corner of Scotland, concerning himself with weighty socio-economic matters that he would write about in a dirge which, 60 years later, would be recited by a ten-year-old in a Dunfermline classroom.

> *See, yonder poor, o'er-labour'd wight,*
> *So abject, mean and vile,*
> *Who begs a brother of the earth*
> *To give him leave to toil;*

Oldest known engraving of the Burns family cottage

And see his lordly fellow-worm,
The poor petition spurn,
Unmindful tho' a weeping wife
And helpless offspring mourn.

If I'm design'd yon lordling's slave,
By Nature's law design'd,
Why was an independent wish
E'er planted in my mind?
If not, why am I subject to
His cruelty or scorn?
Or why has Man the will and pow'r
To make his fellow mourn?

One wonders if the boy Carnegie rose to the indignant levels
Burns intended and, if so, even as a boy, did he respond to them?
Certainly there is no doubt that much of it would have been
relevant to any weaver's child.

Yet let not this too much, my Son,
Disturb thy youthful breast;
This partial view of humankind
Is surely not the last!
The poor, oppressed, honest man
Had never, sure, been born,
Had there not been some recompense
To comfort those that mourn.

Never was a penny better spent.

Robert Burns was so efficient and tactful in offering words to the young, it is easy to forget that these same words were written by one who was still a young man himself. Such are the gifts of prodigy. Carnegie had this same kind of precocity, but as Burns warns in his 'Epistle to a Young Friend':

> *Ye'll try the world soon, my lad,*
> *And, Andrew dear, believe me,*
> *Ye'll find mankind an unco squad*
> *And muckle they may grieve ye:*
> *...*
>
> *I'll no' say men are villains a';*
> *The real, harden'd wicked,*
> *Wha hae nae check but human law*
> *Are tae a few restricket:*
> *But och, mankind are unco weak*
> *An' little to be trusted,*
> *If self the wavering balance shake,*
> *It's rarely right adjusted!*

Inner Circles

Andrew Carnegie well knew the intrinsic value of the self and he was to show in adulthood that he was a more than ordinary man. He was, in fact, a veritable life force. He was energy personified and for him much of that energy was drawn from his mother.

Margaret Carnegie

There's hardly a son doesn't love his own mother, but Carnegie positively worshipped his. Edinburgh-born Margaret Morrison married William Carnegie in 1834, and became the dynamo of the household, running a small shop from the family home and cobbling shoes to help make ends meet. Her resourcefulness and stoic imperturbability in the face of every kind of domestic and family disappointment were a profound influence on her first son, who always held her in a degree of awe. In later life he referred to the bond between them: 'I feel her to be sacred to myself... and not for others to know. None could ever really know her – I alone did that.'

He dedicated his first book, *An American Four-in-Hand in Britain*, published in London in 1883, to 'My Favorite Heroine, My Mother'. There is no doubt that Andrew Carnegie was proud of the courageous and enterprising Margaret Carnegie. In speaking of her in the book, he quotes a couplet from 'The Vision' by Burns:

> *Her eye, even turned on empty space,*
> *Beamed keen with honour...*

Carnegie's love for his mother was further underlined during his triumphant return to his birthplace in Dunfermline in September 1909, when he wrote in the new Memorial Cottage Visitors' Book: 'The humble home of honest poverty. Best heritage of all when one has a heroine for a mother.' When Carnegie eventually did marry, well into middle age, he did so after his mother had died. His only child, a daughter, was named Margaret. What else? He summed up his female relationships himself when he said, 'Two women, my mother and my wife, have made me all that I am.'

Mother fixation was not a trait he shared with Burns. Burns was much closer to his father, William, whom he loved and admired; he rarely mentioned his mother, Agnes, and never wrote to, or about her. After the death of her husband in 1784, Agnes Burnes (the original spelling of the family name) chose to go and live with her second son, Gilbert, at Bolton, near Haddington. She outlived her famous son by a quarter of a century, enjoying the annuity of £5 provided by him. She is not known to have talked much of Robert, even though the rest of Scotland did by the end of his brief life. When she died, Agnes was buried beside Gilbert.

Carnegie, too, had a brother. Tom was, like Gilbert Burns, forever in the shadow of his elder brother. He was not without his own talent but his reputation was never to match that of his whirlwind elder sibling. Their father, William, was a quiet, serious, reticent man with a good brain and pleasant tenor voice whose passions were for politics, his family and reading. He had a deep religious conviction. On one occasion, however, when he and Andrew were attending a church service in Dunfermline, the minister declared that children who were not baptised at birth faced the prospect of everlasting hell. Andrew's baby sister Anne having died in infancy, this was intolerable. Father and son rose and walked out of the church.

There is record of Carnegie's attending Emanuel Swedenborg's scientific and philosophical lay gatherings in Dunfermline and Pittsburgh; he even joined their choir, but conventional piety was not his forte. He found satisfaction in being with free thinkers. This was something he admired in the ideas of Burns. Carnegie said, 'did he not see in advance of his fellows the certain growth of the rights of man through the spread of democracy, and was he not awake to the crude and repulsive theology of his day?'

'The humble
home of honest
poverty. Best heritage
of all when one
has a heroine for
a mother.'

ANDREW CARNEGIE

'The poor, oppressed,
honest man

Had never, sure,
been born,

Had there not been
some recompense

To comfort those
that mourn.'

ROBERT BURNS

Andrew Carnegie was gregarious and always enjoyed good company, just as Burns did. Both men treasured friendship as a necessary currency and Carnegie was later in life to confirm this, idealistically and practically. As Burns put it, 'Should auld acquaintance be forgot, and never brought to mind?'

Carnegie kept faith with his small circle of close friends (the 'Veterans', as his future wife was to call them). Not to diminish his undoubted love for the American-born Louise Whitfield, to whom he owed so much from a personal point of view, the triumvirate of influences – the 'Vets', the mother and the poet – represent a crucial driving force behind Carnegie's achievements.

The Carnegie Veterans represented the 50-year bond he had with some of the workmates and associates he met with in his meteoric rise from the boy-messenger's cubby-hole to the boardrooms of the elite. He lost some partners in his long business life, but he never lost a friend. As Burns wrote of the gift of friendship in the Introduction to his second Commonplace Book:

> I don't know how it is with the world in general, but with me, making remarks is by no means a solitary pleasure. I want someone to laugh with me, to be grave with me, someone to please me and help my discrimination with his or her own remark, and at times, no doubt, to admire my acuteness and penetration…

Carnegie had enormous loyalty to his Vets and as he went up in the world, he took as many of them with him as he could. There were always jobs for the 'boys' as he liked to call them. At their inaugural Veterans' annual New York dinner in the first decade of the 20th century, 41 old men agreed to meet in friendship till the last of them should die. Theirs was a tontine comradeship of survival as found between old soldiers. Carnegie and the Vets had known the best and worst of days and the bonds between them held. 'Rather this, minus fortune, than multi-millionairedom without it – yes, a thousand times, yes.'

Both sides of the Carnegie/Morrison family had this same cultural courage and, in addition, boasted an impressive political resonance. Their genes were undeniably a vivid red. Grandfather Andrew was a keen orator and the recognised leader of the local radical party. Carnegie's other grandfather was a prosperous leather merchant in Edinburgh whose fortunes waned after Waterloo and whose wife died leaving him with eight children to support. His second daughter was Margaret, who inherited her father's resourcefulness and her mother's love of story and song.

Carnegie's republican outlook was shaped by both sides of his family, but especially his father's, who were noted Chartists (so called because of the People's Charter which held out for a voting franchise for all). They were strongly opposed to the idea that Parliamentary representation was the sole privilege of landowners and the aristocracy. That young Carnegie readily absorbed these egalitarian principles was shown in 1902, when he bought Pittencrieff Park in Dunfermline and presented it as a free gift in perpetuity to the people of the town. The gift was influenced no doubt by the fact that he had been excluded as a boy from the very same ground on account of his family's radical views.

Interestingly, Pittencrieff House, which stands in the centre of the park, is where Sir John Forbes lived as a boy. Born in 1707, Forbes grew up to be a general in the British Army of his day and served in the war against the revolutionists in the American colonies. Sir John helped found the city of Pittsburgh which, 200 years later, became Carnegie's first American home and the eventual capital of his industrial empire.

However, the purchase of Pittencrieff Park gave him another connection, one that took him back to his own childhood. He now had a medieval tower and a title, the Laird of Pittencrieff. He liked the relationship it offered to the much earlier Sir Patrick Spens and the poem which begins:

> *The king sat in Dunfermline tower,*
> *Drinking the bluid-red wine...*

(Carnegie was insistent on 'tower' rather than the more usual 'toun' in the wording of the ballad.)

Homestead Strikes

While the gifting of Pittencrieff Park was an undoubted pleasure, Carnegie's meteoric career was not without its darker elements. His reputation was damaged by an incident at the pinnacle of his success: the Homestead Strike. At the end of June 1892, trouble began at the Carnegie-owned Homestead Steel Works near Pittsburgh. Following the introduction of improved machinery, the manager, Henry Frick, had sought to impose a new contract on the Homestead labour force. This move was strongly resisted by the

FRANK LESLIE'S
ILLUSTRATED
WEEKLY

HOMESTEAD TROUBLES.

NEW YORK, JULY 14, 1892.

[Price 10 Cents.]

Amalgamated Association of Iron and Steel Workers, an elite group of skilled workers eager to preserve their status and pay rate relative to the far greater number of unskilled employees at the plant. Talks failed and fights broke out among the workers. When production was brought to a standstill Frick contacted Carnegie, who was in London at the time, by telegram. Carnegie's advice was to keep talking and avoid confrontation because 'No steel is worth an ounce of blood.' However, it is generally considered that Carnegie played too passive a role in what was to become a bloody episode.

Frick was keen to bring in outside workers but the employees drove them out and presented a united front to their employers. They seized the factory and production ceased. It must be remembered that there was then no precedent for this sort of industrial action. Weeks went by and both sides were at stalemate. Frick grew desperate. The strike was now almost on the scale of a military operation.

When townspeople, including women and children, began to move into the factory to assist the union takeover, Frick called in the Pinkerton National Detective Agency. Three hundred armed men arrived by boat. They were met by rifle fire and nine people were killed. The detectives were driven off but returned later that night and there were further fatalities. Frick appealed to Governor Pattison who ordered the state militia to the scene and the superior government force won the day.

Order was fully restored by August and the factory resumed as normal. The unions were defeated and the Amalgamated Association of Iron and Steel Workers was heard of no more. None of its members was tried in the civil courts, though some of the

Striking steel workers ▶

other workers received sentences of up to seven years in prison. There were no unions at Homestead for the next 40 years. A museum now stands on the site, carrying a sign which bears the US Steel logo, and says: 'In Honor of the Workers'.

It is interesting to note that, for some, it is this episode that defines Andrew Carnegie as a ruthless capitalist and that the entire sum of his remarkable philanthropy does not alter their view. One wonders whether Carnegie had cause to reflect on a line of Burns he referred to as 'a rule of life – a pure gem': 'Thine own reproach alone do fear.'

Carnegie the Autodidact

Unlike Burns, Carnegie is not known as a romantic figure, although he wrote many love letters and there is no denying he could be passionate. For example, he retained his reverence for words and provided funds to build 2,811 libraries across the world, with the stipulation that a Burns bust be displayed in each. This was not entirely complied with, but the intention was admirable. He also donated nearly 8,000 church organs to congregations throughout Britain and the United States, saying, 'The happiness of giving is far sweeter than the pleasure direct.' A man of iron and steel he may have been, but the heart of Andrew Carnegie was warm. From Burns' 'First Epistle to Davie' he learned that:

> *Nae treasures, nor pleasures,*
> *Could make us happy lang,*
> *The heart ay's the part ay*
> *That makes us richt or wrang.*

Carnegie was an avid consumer of art and music and confessed that 'with songs and tunes I am as fickle as Burns was with his favourite lassies; one queen gives place to another with surprising facility'. Of his favourite Burns' song, 'My Nanie's Awa', he felt it was 'a shame to quote any part of it, because every line seems a necessary step leading higher and higher until the region of fire is entered'.

Carnegie never ceased to appreciate the good things in life – good talk, good companionship and good work at all levels. He advocated the spread of the written word with almost missionary fervour: books had been his first release and his many library bequests were meant as a gesture of thanks.

It was due to the availability of books at crucial stages in his own life that he himself became the formidable man so vividly depicted in the museum housed in the Dunfermline weaver's cottage where he was born in 1835. Virtually self-taught, self-made and self-assured from the start, Carnegie was a typical Victorian autodidact, climbing life's ladder on the rungs of his own initiative, buoyed by a wide reading of books and men. His first contact with literature was when his father started an informal library for his fellow weavers and he helped carry books in William's large weaver's apron. Who is to say that the lad didn't steal a look at the volumes as they passed through his hands, giving him his lifelong love of the written word and a deep instinct to better himself? He once noted, 'As the twig is bent, so is the tree inclined.'

The scholarly bent, as one might say, was on his father's side. It was already in his redoubtable grandfather and namesake, Andrew Carnegie of Pattiesmuir, who was dubbed 'The Professor' by his contemporaries due to his leadership of an informal debating club called the 'Pattiesmuir College'. Grandfather Carnegie was a lively one by all accounts, one 'auld wifie' describing him fondly as 'that daft callant, Andra Carnegie'. It must have been he who gave Carnegie his sense of fun. Didn't the grandson believe with some certainty that a sunny disposition was worth more than any fortune? As he said, 'The mind like the body can be moved from the shade into the sunshine. Let us move it then.' Although he also said that 'many a weary anxious hour has the search for [Burns'] gems [brought me] to something like calm', so perhaps he did not always enjoy such perfect equilibrium.

Carnegie's uncle, George Lauder, was married to his mother's sister, Seaton Morrison, and kept a shop in Dunfermline. He had a mind packed full of Scottish history and quirky facts, and was fond of telling young Andrew that 'if Scotland's mountains were rolled out flat, she would be bigger than England!' Lauder was an educated man and his nephew was grateful for his unique insights. George recognised that every boy needs a hero and sold 'Naig' (as he called Andrew) the vision of Wallace and Bruce which gave him what he called his 'vein of Scottish patriotism'.

Uncle Lauder also taught him the names of the kings and queens of England by telling him to imagine each monarch in a certain place in the room, to which he would point. In this way, Carnegie always saw King John sign the Magna Carta on the mantelpiece and Victoria with her children all about her on the back of the front door. Carnegie may indeed have had a photographic memory, a vital tool in his later work on the telegraph and another reason for his rapid rise in the workforce. He listened and he remembered.

Burns had the same gift of memory. John Murdoch taught the 12-year-old farmer's son French by pointing out features in the home and asking Burns to repeat their names. After only two weeks, Burns was reading French. People too often forget that Burns, the supposed ploughman-poet, had an educated brain.

It is only right that such an important influence in Carnegie's life as George Lauder should be remembered in Lauder Technical College, part of the present-day Fife College, also Carnegie's gift to the town. However, it was to the poet Burns that Andrew Carnegie was to look for his greatest life inspiration. He found in Scotland's bard all the echoes of his own nationalism and the folk sense of Scotland that he learned at his mother's knee.

It was while Carnegie was staying at Skibo Castle in 1909 that this Burns connection was recognised by his being made an Honorary Vice-President of the Burns Federation, along with no less than the renowned Burns speaker, Lord Rosebery. Editions of Burns were often dedicated to Carnegie during his lifetime, especially in the United States.

It has already been mentioned that Carnegie personally stipulated that a Burns bust should be installed in every one of his libraries. One was also installed in the Wallace Monument in Stirling in recognition of Burns' often-stated patriotism, a quality shared by Carnegie, who wrote in his *Autobiography*:

> Ruskin truly observes that every bright boy born in Edinburgh is influenced by the sight of the Castle. So is the child of Dunfermline, by its noble Abbey, the Westminster of Scotland, founded early in the

11th century by Malcolm Canmore and his Queen, Margaret, Scotland's patron saint... Fortunate, indeed, the child who first sees the light in that romantic town, which occupies high ground three miles north of the Firth of Forth, overlooking the sea, with Edinburgh in sight to the south, and to the north the peaks of the Ochils clearly in view. All is still redolent of the mighty past when Dunfermline was both nationally and religiously the capital of Scotland.

Carnegie on Burns

Carnegie's shrewd appreciation of Burns' skill as a writer was intensified in 1886 when, during his convalescence from typhoid, he turned to his beloved books, and of course, to Burns. One can imagine him at this time deeply pondering the nature of genius in literature, which he would later describe as 'the power to lead an understanding and sympathetic reader step by step, line after line, into regions more and more elevated, stirring the heart'.

To encapsulate a big thought in a few words was to Carnegie the sign of Burns' poetic genius and in an essay written during his recovery he provides examples of this word 'economy', of so much content bought with so few words spent. His first example is from 'The Twa Dogs':

> When rural life, o' ev'ry station,
> Unite in common recreation;
> Love blinks, Wit slaps, an' social Mirth
> Forgets there's Care upon the earth...

Carnegie with his dog 'Laddie' at Skibo Castle ▶

...

The canty auld folks crackin' crouse,
The young anes rantin' thro' the house –
My heart has been sae fain to see them,
That I for joy hae barkit wi' them.

Everything in the verse is in that last line. According to Carnegie, it tells us that the dog is one of the family, as the collie was in every peasant home and not beneath the notice of the poet. For Carnegie this is what distinguishes Burns from the merely talented. Carnegie also recognises that Burns, like Milton, had a partiality for the Devil, for whom he had several names, Auld Hangie, Auld Cloots, as in his 'Address to the Deil':

An' now, Auld Cloots, I ken you're thinkin',
A certain Bardie's rantin', drinkin',
Some luckless hour will send him linkin'
To your black pit;
But, faith! he'll turn a corner jinkin',
An' cheat you yet.

In Burns' opinion, even Satan has every chance of redemption. The glow of sympathy for the Fallen Angel is all-pervading, and, if he could, Burns would even do the Devil a good turn.

Quoting the leading literary critic of the day, Matthew Arnold, Carnegie is like-minded in thinking that for dramatic force nothing equals 'Tam o' Shanter' outside the works of Shakespeare. Of the scene in Alloway Kirk with witches and warlocks in a dance, Arnold comments:

The masterstroke here is in giving the Devil the role of the piper, for without music no dance is possible. This gets to the very root of the matter... Those who dance must pay the piper... and the last touch, the 'little more' that makes all the difference – mirth and revelry – life at the flood in a ring lit by candles held in the hands of the dead. The element of the awful is thus introduced with appalling power.

For Carnegie, a dog lover, one of the most attractive qualities about Burns was his insistence that love is in all things, for all things. Even in sheep, when he puts words into the mouth of the dying 'Poor Mailie', the poet's pet ewe:

And now, my bairns, wi' my last braith,
I lea'e my blessin' wi' you baith,
And when you think upo' your mither,
Mind to be kind to ane anither.

Carnegie calls this 'a sermon in two lines for every family in the world'. In Burns' 'The Vision', the poet is told to 'preserve the dignity of man with soul erect' before the Spirit herself 'like a passing thought... fled in light away'. Carnegie considers this an exquisitely delicate ending to Burns' finest work, and those two words, 'in light', an inspiration. In considering the famous 'To a Mouse', he sees it as an illustration of one of Burns' tenets, that 'all flesh is kin'. He also sees the importance of 'John Anderson, my Jo', converted by Burns from a piece of pornography into the perfect metaphor for two hearts living as one in a long marriage where everything is shared, even the prospect of eternity.

Then there was what Thomas Carlyle calls 'the war-hymn of the ages', 'Scots Wha Hae', which Burns himself knew would stand for all time, just like his song of fellowship, 'Auld Lang Syne'. It's hard to believe that such a wide-ranging, deeply felt canon of work came from a young man of 25, hardly begun in the world. In Carnegie's judgement, this is explicable only by the law of Genius. The self-taught Carnegie was fascinated by Burns' skill: 'Did Burns painfully think that out? Muse over it? Labor away at that part of it or this part of it? Or did the idea flash upon him like a stroke of lightning?'

He ends his essay with what he calls the Hymn of Triumphant Democracy encapsulated in a couplet from 'Is there, For Honest Poverty', with which Burns, with true poetic insight, proclaims the Brotherhood of Man.

> *Then let us pray that come it may –*
> *As come it will for a' that –*
> *That sense and worth, o'er a' the earth,*
> *May bear the gree, and a' that;*
> *For a' that, and a' that,*
> *It's comin' yet for a' that,*
> *That man to man, the warld o'er,*
> *Shall brithers be for a' that.*

A Natural Businessman

The enthusiasm Carnegie evinced for Burns' poetry was typical of the vigour with which he tackled many things in his life – even boyhood chores. Fetching the family's water from the well, the young Carnegie

Carnegie's uncle, George Lauder ▶

often jumped the queue of women: they thought him 'an awfu laddie'. Later, when his mother started a 'wee shop' in their cottage, he became her eager keeper of accounts. In this way, still only ten, he was introduced to rudimentary business methods.

When Robert Burns was ten he was learning about doing without meat on the table. At 12 he was walking into Ayr for his French lessons with Mr Murdoch just as Carnegie at the same age went to his Uncle Lauder's home for history lessons. Thus, two thirsty young minds were drinking as much from the fountain of knowledge as they could gulp down.

The future czar of the steel mills was hinted at even at primary school. His mother thought it a good idea to have some pets around the house as the best means of keeping Andrew and his young brother, Tom, 'in the right path', as she said. She had her husband build a hutch at the back of their home and left the care of the rabbits entirely to young 'Andra'. It was here that he experienced what he called 'my first business venture': he co-opted his classmates to bring in food for the animals in return for having baby rabbits named after them. He was to write of his first lesson in management:

> My conscience reproves me today, looking back, when
> I think of the hard bargain I drove with my young
> playmates, many of whom were content to gather
> dandelions and clover for a whole season with me,
> conditioned upon this unique reward – the poorest
> return ever made to labor. Alas! what else had I to
> offer them? Not a penny.

◀ Robert Burns, painted in 1787 by Alexander Nasmyth
now owned by the National Galleries of Scotland

We have seen how firmly the Burns root was planted in the Carnegie psyche. If we can keep this in mind and remember the near century rolling on between them we might better understand the parallels in the lives of two very different men. Each had a hard beginning in life yet neither doubted that he was capable of better things. This gave them the doggedness and determination to win clear of their respective situations and to this end they applied themselves with intense dedication. Both were ruthless in pursuit of their goals, the main one being to avoid poverty. Nothing focuses the mind more than the prospect of dereliction. Reading was to prove their salvation. Every line read was a window to the wider world beyond their home environment and each grasped at the view the page offered.

Travel for Carnegie and Burns

Their common aim was to achieve the security in which they could work at their own thing. Deep down, Carnegie was as creative as much as Burns was a worker. Witness the sheer number of words Burns committed to paper in his writing life of a mere score of years. And with a goose quill! Like Carnegie he was an example of industry allied to a natural talent and abnormal energy.

In 1786, Burns had no place to call his own, having given up his share of Mossgiel Farm to brother Gilbert in exchange for his looking after Burns' illegitimate daughter by Lizzie Paton. Added to this, he had to hide from the warrant put out by James Armour for his arrest on account of Jean Armour's twins. One of the great ironies of the Burns story is that he only went into print in order to earn his passage money to the West Indies to become what was then called 'a negro driver'. In all likelihood, his only thought was to escape the possibility of prison. He did so by paying off Armour from the royalties due on his first book of poems (his only book, as it happened) and at the same time leaving some money with the family at Mossgiel. That done, he would be off. Then, 'Farewell, Scotland, I shall never see you more...'

He was stopped from the August sailing of the *Nancy* under Captain Smith by the overwhelming success of the original Kilmarnock Edition which quickly caused old Armour to withdraw his writ. Nevertheless, Burns, just to be sure, transferred his nine guinea passage to the *Bell* under Captain Cathcart, due to sail from Greenock in September.

By this time, a certain Dr Blacklock wrote to Burns' patron in Ayrshire, suggesting that Burns should try for a second edition in Edinburgh, which Burns said was almost as foreign to him as Jamaica. This posed an immediate dilemma for the would-be poet; to try for an Edinburgh edition or to cross the Atlantic. He chose to publish and the Bell sailed without him. What few people know is that Burns made a third Atlantic reservation on the *Roselle* under Captain Hogg, due to sail from Leith on 10 November just in case Edinburgh did not work out, he was taking no chances. In 'To Mary Campbell' he wrote:

> *Will ye go to the Indies, my Mary,*
> *And leave auld Scotia's shore?*
> *Will ye go to the Indies, my Mary,*
> *Across th'Atlantic's roar?*

Such was the sensation of his first year in Edinburgh that the *Roselle* also sailed without Burns. He toured the Borders instead, savouring his new-won fame. The decision to publish rather than sail was obviously a wise one; the Edinburgh edition of his poems sold him to all of Scotland, then to London and, from there, to the world where he has remained ever since.

If Burns had made his name by letting three ships go sailing by, Carnegie's future was defined by his family's decision in May 1848 to take one out of Glasgow bound for America. Burns made £20 out of his original Kilmarnock Edition, exactly the amount the Carnegies were short of for their Atlantic passage. Fortunately, Margaret Carnegie was friendly with Ella Ferguson who had been the midwife at Andrew's birth and now, as Mrs Henderson, kept a baker's shop in St Margaret Street, Dunfermline. She loaned the family the necessary sum with Uncle Lauder acting as guarantor.

It is therefore Mrs Henderson we should thank for the phenomenon that became Andrew Carnegie, just as we should thank the blind Dr Blacklock for putting the idea of Edinburgh in Burns' mind and deflecting him from emigration. Carnegie became a legend because he crossed the Atlantic, Burns became an icon because he didn't.

It took Burns two days on a hired pony to canter across the Lowlands from Mossgiel Farm to the High Street of Edinburgh. It took the Carnegies three months to go west. First a carriage from Dunfermline to Charlestown on the Forth and then on the Clyde Canal by barge to Glasgow to board the *Wiscasset*, an ex-whaler bound for New York. It was then by steamboat via Lake Erie and its canals and the River Ohio to arrive finally at the home of his

The Wiscasset, engraved onto a whale tooth

mother's twin sisters, Annie and Kittie, in Pittsburgh, Pennsylvania. Burns' 'Epistle to a Young Friend' still seems apt:

> *To catch Dame Fortune's golden smile,*
> *Assiduous wait upon her;*
> *And gather gear by ev'ry wile,*
> *That's justified by honour;*
> *Not for to hide it in a hedge,*
> *Nor for a train-attendant;*
> *But for the glorious privilege*
> *Of being independent.*
> *...*
>
> *In ploughman phrase, 'God send you speed,'*
> *Still daily to grow wiser;*
> *And may ye better reck the rede,*
> *Than ever did th'adviser!*

Before the ship sailed from Glasgow, Andrew had to be pulled away from the neck of his beloved Uncle Lauder by a sailor, one Robert Barryman. It was a sad parting. The seven-week Atlantic segment was a nightmare for everyone on board except the 12-year-old Carnegie. He made a friend of the same Robert Barryman who got him a job on deck helping the crew. This may have led to young Andrew's being able to get hold of extra provisions for his family below decks. If so, it was a further indication of his enterprise. The plum duff and fresh water given to him by the crew might have provided much-needed nourishment on a crossing that saw many perish.

However bad conditions may have been in the overcrowded ship, whether on deck or in steerage, they were not as obscenely awful as they were for the thousands of poor Africans who had sailed not so very long before to become slaves in the same sugar plantations for which Burns had been intended. The mature Carnegie was appalled by the slavery practised in the southern states of America, and would indeed have been horrified had his hero, Burns, really become a 'negro driver'.

The excitement of landing in New York overwhelmed the boy Carnegie, but almost the first person he met in the city was Able Seaman Barryman. The kindly sailor, now dressed in 'regular Jack-ashore fashion in white jacket and blue trousers' was, as Carnegie put it, 'the most beautiful man I had ever seen... my ideal Tom Bowling.' Barryman hoisted him up on his back and took him off to a refreshment stand where he bought the boy a large brass jug of sarsaparilla. This was his welcome to the New World. It was a good omen. Years later Carnegie tried to trace Barryman but without success. Exhausted and covered in mosquito bites, the Carnegie quartet finally arrived at their first home in America, two rooms above their Aunt Aitken's shop at 336½ Rebecca Street in Allegheny City, near Pittsburgh. The family lived upstairs while William Carnegie wove his exquisite damask linen on a loom on the ground floor. Without agents in America, William had to sell his cloth directly from door to door. He was a skilled weaver, but no salesman. Margaret Carnegie, as usual, came to the rescue with her cobbling and sewing skills and the Carnegies survived.

Andrew offered to peddle his father's work along the wharves but his mother would not hear of it. To her it felt too much like vagrancy. William was therefore forced to sell the handloom and work as a labourer in a cotton mill run by an old Scotsman, Mr Blackstock. Even so, the father got a job for his son at the same factory. It was now all hands to the mill for the Carnegies if they were to find elbow room for themselves in this new country. Andrew began as a bobbin boy for $1.20 per week and he hated it, being stifled indoors with only a steam boiler for company. He had to get a better job and in 1850 he did, being hired as a telegraph messenger boy for the O'Reilly Telegraph Company.

Being Carnegie, he became the top boy in no time and, observing the operators at work, made himself a proficient operator. So much so he was paid an extra $2 a day which, he wrote later, 'gave me greater pleasure than all the millions I've made since'. By 1852, he was earning more than his father. However, the father was still shown in the son when Andrew himself petitioned Colonel Anderson of Pittsburgh to let him become a 'working boy' borrower at his private library. This was granted and the 16-year-old, with many other lads, took full advantage of this access to books. He also took the chance to see his first train, attend his first theatre on a free pass and see his first Shakespeare play. Every new experience was grist to his mill.

At the same age, Burns was composing his first song to a girl, a fellow harvester in the field. 'I never had the least inclination of thought of turning Poet till I got heartily in Love,' he writes in his First Commonplace Book (1783), 'and then Rhyme and Song were, in a manner, the spontaneous language of my heart.' Andrew Carnegie had no time to fall in love because he now had a mother and wee brother to keep. His shy, reticent father had never been a man of the world. 'He was all over for Heaven,' as his son put it. He died in 1855 at the age of 51. Like Burns' 'Vision', he 'fled in light away'.

William Burnes, the father of Robert Burns, died aged 64 on Mount Oliphant farm, similarly broken by overwork and undernourishment and fretting only for his wayward son. 'It's only you I fret for' he said before he died. Burns bitterly mourned his good father. He entered into a new farm at Mossgiel with his brother Gilbert 'full of resolution' but instead became better known in the district as 'a maker of rhyme and unashamed lover of the female sex'. He also became a Deputy Master of the St James Masonic Lodge.

The Rise of Andrew Carnegie

Bearing in mind his status as man of the house, Carnegie knew he had to inch himself up the commercial ladder. This he did, in 1853, by becoming personal telegraph operator to the superintendent of the Pittsburgh Division of the Pennsylvania Railroad Company, Thomas A Scott. Scott invited him to become his confidential secretary at $35 a month, an opportunity young Andrew seized with both hands.

While still a telegraph operator, Carnegie joined the Webster Literary Society along with the 'trusty five', as he called his inner group of friends, all fellow messengers: Dave McCargo, Bob Pitcairn, Tom Miller, John Phipps and William Cowley. They were to be the 'Veterans' of his last years. They joined the Webster to learn something of self-possession before an audience, how to talk *to* them and not *at* them and never to *orate* at any time. The boys went on to form their own debating club in the cobbler's room provided by John Phipps' father. It was yet another chance for Carnegie to learn. It appears that he spoke for an hour and half one

◀ The old building at the corner of Third and Wood Streets, Pittsburgh, where Andrew Carnegie became a telegraph messenger in 1849

evening on the motion 'Should a judiciary be elected by the people?'

His experience at the Webster evokes Burns' formation of the Tarbolton Bachelors' Club in 1780, with a handful of friends as 'a diversion to relieve the wearied man worn down with the necessary labours of life'. However, there is nothing to suggest that Carnegie and the 'trusty five' would have been inclined to stipulate, as the young Burns and his close friends did, 'That every member of this society should love one, or more, of the opposite sex.' Burns lived for love and verse-making and, as he admitted, 'was easily roused to both'. Young Carnegie, on the other hand, chased every chance to prosper.

The first came when Mr Scott invited him to make an investment in the new Adams Express Company (now American Express) by purchasing ten shares for $600. This was an enormous sum, but Carnegie agreed. To help raise the money, Margaret Carnegie, with her brother's help, remortgaged the house bought with all the spare cash pulled in by the family since they had arrived in the United States and now kept safely in a long stocking. It was from this same piece of hosiery that she repaid Mrs Henderson. Lending her elder son $500 was no risk to Margaret Carnegie. She knew well the solid rock on which he was built. On receiving his first monthly dividend cheque for $10 from Adams Express, Carnegie apparently exclaimed, 'Eureka, here's the goose that lays the golden egg!' Not yet 20, he had taken the first step on the road that was to make him the richest man in the world by the end of the century.

Carnegie's career proceeded on smooth rails with only one incident to disturb progress. This was when 'Mr Scott's Andy' set out from Altoona to Pittsburgh with the week's payroll to pay the men on the

Railroad executive Thomas A Scott ▶

new railroad site. Being train mad, he chose to ride up on the engine with the driver. Such was the bumping on the rough track that the bulky package supposedly secure under his waistcoat worked clear, bouncing out of the speeding train and onto the side of the track. Carnegie had to use all his powers of talk to persuade the train driver to brake and reverse until they found the payroll packet lying on the bank only a matter of feet from the river.

'God, you were lucky, Andy,' said the train driver.

Lucky Andy he was.

'Do your duty, and a little more, and the future will take care of itself' is another Carnegie motif. He proved it when in 1859, aged only 24, he was appointed superintendent of the Western Division of the Pennsylvania Railroad Company on a salary of $1,500 per year. His younger brother Tom was appointed as his private secretary. He and Andrew could now wear kid gloves. We hear little of Tom Carnegie, yet he went on to play a large part in his brother's success, some say a key part.

Tom married early and was a committed family man having no fewer than nine children with his wife Lucy. He later bought an island – Cumberland, off the Atlantic coast – with his own considerable fortune and on it built each of the children a house of their own. Sadly, Tom Carnegie was to die an alcoholic aged just 43.

Margaret Carnegie, however, more than got her money back from her investment in her first son. Carnegie bought his aunt's house for $700 and installed his mother there. She was in her own house again and Andrew was delighted for her. Margaret was still

all things to him – mother, teacher and inspiration – in one tiny, down-to-earth, practical Scotswoman. Nothing rattled her, except having servants in the house. When the Carnegies later bought their first big house with its own grounds in Altoona, far enough from Pittsburgh to be clear of its constant soot, it took her some time to get used to having servants in the house.

The first real illness he had ever known in his life and the necessary leave of absence it gave him from the railway, allowed Carnegie to take his mother and brother back to Dunfermline for the first time since their emigration. How different the return voyage? In 1862, Carnegie took his hometown by storm at exactly the same age Burns was when he was the sensation in Edinburgh in 1787. Burns wrote to Gilbert then: 'My name is on every lip... I am the game and gossip of the day, the darling of my lady's salon, the wonder of all the gay world!'

The 27-year-old Carnegie did not wax so lyrical but there was no denying he was in a dream. As promised, his mother came back in her own carriage. One old aunt thought he looked as prosperous as if he owned a shop in the High Street. He could have bought the whole street! He had no such aim of course. He was so moved that all he wanted to do was kneel down and kiss the ground on which he stood.

Yet his first impression was that the Dunfermline town and all its townsfolk had shrunk. Everything was in miniature. 'It's a city of Lilliputians!' he exclaimed. His own modest height belied the big man-of-the-world he had become. He was now a star-spangled American, a man who had met and worked with Abraham Lincoln.

Burns had likewise met with the great and good of his own day. He returned west in 1788 like a conquering hero, following his prince-like progress through the Borders and around the Highlands, selling his book at every dinner table by entertaining the guests with excerpts. Now it was time to settle down. He married the loyal Jean Armour in Mauchline and built his own farmhouse at Ellisland near Dumfries. People thought he had retired. Unlike Carnegie, Burns felt that ruin was always snapping at his heels. A sinecure was arranged for him from Edinburgh in the Excise Service in Dumfries which would allow him plenty of time for writing and keep his family in some comfort. But, for some reason, the required papers never reached Dumfries.

He did indeed enrol in government service, although not as a comfortable pen in an office but in the uniform of a humble part-time exciseman who had to provide his own horse.

> *But what d'ye think, my trusty fier?*
> *I'm turned a gauger – Peace be here*
> *Parnassian queries, I fear, I fear,*
> *Ye'll noo disdain me,*
> *And then my 50 pounds a year*
> *Will little gain me.*

His new part-time Customs duties were added to his part-time farming, the first paying him a wage and the second providing him with shelter: the security which gave him the opportunity to write what was, in his own view, his masterpiece, 'Tam o' Shanter'.

Carnegie never wrote a literary masterpiece, although his *Gospel of Wealth* was a respected and enduring work in its field. Nor did he wear a uniform. He was actually called up by the Union Army in 1864, the year before the war ended, but like many men who could afford it, he paid an Irish immigrant John Lindew $850 to wear the uniform in his place. This was common practice at the time. Carnegie was very much a sympathiser with the Northern cause in the American Civil War and made no secret of it. He became involved in Unionist communication and transportation system which was how he met Lincoln.

While Robert Burns was very impressed when he was first invited to dine with young Lord Dear, Carnegie admitted to a great timidity in going into other people's houses. The first time he ever spent a night in a strange house was when he visited Mr and Mrs Stokes at their home in Greensberg. Mr Stokes, the lawyer for the Pennsylvania Railroad, had been intrigued by an article Carnegie had written for the *Pittsburgh Journal* on the city's attitude to the new railways. The young superintendent, invited to dinner in order to talk about it, was overawed by the grandeur of the house. He was especially taken with a quotation inscribed on a marble mantel in the library which read:

> *He that cannot reason is a fool,*
> *He that will not is a bigot,*
> *He that dare not, a slave.*

Carnegie vowed to have such an inscription in his own library one day. He later did just that when it was placed on the wall in Skibo Castle.

At a time when massive fortunes were being made across the newly industrialised America, Andrew Carnegie's was to become the biggest of them all. He was his own bank eventually. However he believed that 'no man can become rich without enriching others'.

At 33, in the St Nicholas Hotel, New York, he wrote a memo (a copy of which is on display in the Andrew Carnegie Birthplace

Museum Collection), reminding himself to give up work in two years' time, 'settle in Oxford and get thorough education'. Learning was a passion that governed his whole life and his greatest disappointment latterly, along with his horror of the impending world war, was his failure to obtain a university education as an adult.

The Oxford plan was sidetracked in 1872 by a visit to Britain and a meeting with Henry Bessemer, the inventor of the Bessemer process, a vital factor enabling the mass production of steel. Carnegie had found his second passion outside books and just as thoroughly applied himself to it.

He returned to America, resigned from the Pennsylvania Railway and began investing seriously in steel and all its ramifications. It was this that was to make him a millionaire for the first time and lay the basis for his vast fortune. He made a tour of the world collecting engineering ideas, ideas he implemented as soon as he got back home. He took the best advice wherever he found it and acted on it wholeheartedly. His credo in business was to discover one's line and stick to it. Furnaces and steel mills seemed to grow under his fingers and the dollars rained down on him like confetti.

Married Life

It was now that he finally decided to get married. His engagement to Louise Whitfield, the daughter of a wealthy New York merchant, was postponed no less than three times. It may have been that Margaret Carnegie influenced her son's matrimonial procrastination. Perhaps

Thirty three and an income of 50,000$
per annum,

By this time two years I can so arrange all
my business as to secure at least 50,000 per
annum — Beyond this never earn — make no
effort to increase fortune, but spend the
surplus each year for benevolent purposes,
Cast aside business forever except for
others, —

Settle in Oxford & get a thorough education
making the acquaintance of literary men
this will take three years active work —
pay especial attention to speaking in public,
Settle then in London & purchase a
controlling interest in some Newspaper or
Live review & give the general management
of it attention, taking a part in public
matters especially those connected with
Education & improvement of the poorer
Classes —

Man must have an idol — The amassing
of wealth is one of the worst species of
idolatry — no idol more debasing than the
worship of money — Whatever I engage in I must
push inordinately therefor should I be careful
to choose that life which will be the most elevating
in its character — To continue much longer
overwhelmed by business cares and with most
of my thoughts wholly upon the way to make
more money in the shortest time, must degrade
me beyond hope of permanent recovery,
I will resign business at thirty five, but during
the ensuing two years I wish to spend the afternoons
in receiving instruction, and in reading systematically

Memorandum made in December 1868 in which Andrew Carnegie drew
up a life programme and pledged himself to devote his 'surplus each year
for benevolent purposes'

unsurprisingly, Louise is on record as saying that Carnegie's mother was 'the most unpleasant woman I ever met in my life'.

Carnegie first met Louise at her father's house and he courted her as they went horse riding in Central Park. At the end of 1886, all three Carnegies went down with typhoid fever, possibly caused by the domestic water supply (disease being impervious to wealth). While he was still sick, but on the mend, he was informed of his brother's death, then, a matter of days later, he learned that his mother had also passed away. Carnegie was at his nadir. It was then he was visited by Miss Whitfield, who was shocked to see him brought so low. She encouraged him back to health and life and six months later on 22 April 1887, Carnegie, 51, and Louise, 22 years his junior, were married. He was far from his peak but he was possibly as happy as he had ever been.

In 1895, Louise bought from William Templeman the Dunfermline cottage in which Carnegie had been born and gave it to her husband as a 60th birthday present. The cottage was eventually opened to the public in 1908 and, with further additions and improvements over the years, it still stands proudly as the Andrew Carnegie Birthplace Museum.

Margaret Carnegie, the second, arrived on 30 March 1897 and a year later her father bought and restored Skibo Castle on the Dornoch Firth for the family. The Visitors' Book there was soon to include the name of everyone who was anyone, including King Edward VII, Queen Victoria's son, who offered Carnegie an honour for his services to society. Carnegie felt that to accept would be against his socialist principles and politely declined. He requested that he be sent a simple letter of thanks instead.

Virtually a hundred years before, on 25 July 1796, Robert Burns had been buried with a totally inappropriate military funeral; on that very day, a boy called Maxwell, his 13th child, was born to Jean Armour in the Burns House, Dumfries. Robert Burns died worrying about his family and the small debts he would leave them. He didn't reckon on the debt Scotland owed *him* – the country's gratitude was shown in the national appeal raised for the family after his death.

The six surviving children, three legitimate and three illegitimate, were each set up to enjoy a comfortable, upper-middle class posterity. Burns would have appreciated that. If he did not foresee his countrymen's charity, he certainly knew he would not be forgotten. As he said to his wife in his final year, 'Don't worry, Jean. My name will be known even more a hundred years from now.'

By the hundred years Burns talked about, Andrew Carnegie was Rector of St Andrew's University, heavy with honorary degrees and with the freedom of many cities including the first, his beloved Dunfermline. He was famous and feted far and wide. His greatest talent, however, was his continuing zest for life, his thirst for new experience.

Andrew Carnegie's Philanthropy

Remembering the decision taken at the St Nicholas Hotel when he was a mere 33, based on his view that it is wrong that any man should keep more money than he needs, he decided in 1901 to retain only the minimum required to live. This he now continued

Andrew Carnegie with his daughter Margaret ▶

to do with even greater enthusiasm and, even though his minimum living stipend would be more than a fortune to most, by far the greater balance went in projects for the public good. They still do via the various worldwide Carnegie Trusts. His name has become synonymous with charitable works and generosity.

On Saturday 29 August 1903, Carnegie arrived in Kilmarnock to receive the Freedom of the Burgh and attend a dinner in his honour. During proceedings a certain Bailie William Monroe suggested to their celebrated guest that he might be willing to pay half a million dollars from his reputed 60 million dollar fortune to build a 'Temple to Robert Burns' in the town, featuring statues of Burns and all his associates. Carnegie, who had that day laid the foundation stone for a new school in Loanhead to be built at his expense was not amused.

'You've spoiled my day,' was his only comment.

That was all that was said but the incident quickly passed into rumour which soon became accepted as fact and became sensational news all over Scotland. It spread in no time from New York to New Zealand and back home again to New Cumnock. It caused more than a little stir in Kilmarnock itself. The playful Bailie Monroe, who had mooted the idea as a joke (he claimed), was forced to apologise and himself donated £50 to the Kilmarnock Infirmary.

Needless to say, the Temple was never built. However, the Federation of Burns Clubs (founded in London in 1885) now operates from Kilmarnock as the Robert Burns World Federation and is paid for by Burns lovers all over the world. It is appropriate

that it operates from the place that saw the printing of Burns' only book in 1786.

From this point onwards the man who had more money than anyone since Croesus, decided to spend the rest of his life giving it away. Carnegie's riches would be used to enrich others. Following a mining disaster in Pennsylvania in 1904, he immediately set up the Carnegie Hero Fund Trust which he called 'my ain bairn'. Its aim was to honour ordinary people who had carried out spontaneous acts of heroism and provide some recompense in the form of grants for surviving heroes, or their families.

Carnegie's interest in this work was influenced by his pacifism which stemmed from his own experiences during the American Civil War when he witnessed the terrible and needless loss of life of so many young soldiers in dreadful conditions. He felt it was unjust that the bravery of ordinary civilians was not properly recognised. The Peace Palace in The Hague was largely funded by a £1.5 million donation by Carnegie in an attempt to persuade countries to avoid all future wars. Ironically, it was completed in 1913, only a year before the First World War broke out.

Carnegie's Death and Legacy

Carnegie was so dispirited by seeing his world and its values disappearing all around him that, for the first time in his life, he lost his spirit and vitality. He lost heart and retreated to his new home at Lennox, Massachusetts where he died on 11 August 1919.

He was laid to rest in the Sleepy Hollow Cemetery, Tarrytown, New York. In the end, he died disenchanted by a world torn apart by wars; saddened by the death of most of his friends, it is reported that he said: 'I want to go before there's no one left to call me Andy.'

A few years earlier, Andrew Carnegie had been in London dining with a friend, John Morley. They were discussing William Wordsworth. Carnegie mentioned that Wordsworth, who was born during Burns' lifetime, went to visit the poet's grave in Alloway and wrote about it thus:

I mourned with thousands, but as one
More deeply grieved, for he was gone
Whose light I hailed when first it shone,
And showed my youth

How verse may build a princely throne
On Humble truth
…

We might have been
…

True friends though diversely inclined;
But heart with heart and mind with mind,
Where the main fibres are entwined
Through Nature's skill,
May even by contraries be joined
More closely still.

Wordsworth might have been speaking for Carnegie's relationship with Burns. In mind and heart they shared much, except a long life. Burns never got to be old. Morley said he couldn't recollect any poem in Burns relating to old age. He obviously didn't know 'John Anderson, my Jo', but Carnegie then told him of the epiphany he himself had with Burns and mentioned reciting 'Man Was Made to Mourn' for 'Snuffy Martin' and the whole school for a penny. He then recited the last verse:

> *O Death! the poor man's dearest friend,*
> *The kindest and the best!*
> *Welcome the hour my aged limbs*
> *Are laid with thee at rest!*
> *The great, the wealthy fear thy blow,*
> *From pomp and pleasure torn;*
> *But, oh! a blest relief to those*
> *That weary-laden mourn!*

John Morley promptly handed Carnegie a penny.

Dunfermline today continues to salute her most remarkable son and his extraordinary achievements, his radical ideas and their application in worldwide philanthropy. The great wealth Carnegie accumulated was, and still is, used for the benefit of citizens across the globe. He always held firm to the belief that what a man has done for good in life is the only worthwhile profit made. Andrew Carnegie lived according to that conviction. His legacy lives on.

A Personal Reflection

I have found this 'relationship' between Andrew Carnegie and Robert Burns a fascinating and illuminating discovery. Of the two men, I admit to knowing more of Burns, having portrayed the Bard in a solo play for theatre since 1965 and in the 1968 television biography. Since then, he has been my travelling companion in tours around the world. I have written half a dozen books based on this working connection and I am still frequently asked to talk about his life and works wherever admirers of Robert Burns gather.

My acquaintance with Andrew Carnegie is more recent. Although like most Scots I knew of him and his highly profitable industrial exploits and of the famous Carnegie Hero Fund, it wasn't until 2008, when the Carnegie Dunfermline Trust invited me to record a commentary on his life for their Birthplace Museum, that I got to know him better. Then, in 2011, I gave a lecture on Carnegie's lifetime admiration of Burns. In drafting this speech, I was given access to papers in the Birthplace Museum collection and learned more of his life story.

Burns died young in a delirium, Carnegie died old, at peace with himself, if not with the world. Along with so many other threads of connection, they were united in their sense of disappointment with the world and its unjust ways. Burns had looked to the French Revolution for new hope for the ordinary man, but saw that ideal flame and then burn out in the reign of terror that followed. With the beginnings of industrialisation he saw the end of the weavers' home traditions – this was what sent Carnegie to America, to a new start in a new world, but one of the first things he experienced was a civil war. America brought him the opportunity to achieve success on the back of personal industry.

A man of passionate social ideals, Carnegie was broken-hearted by the outbreak of the First World War in 1914. For the time being, human nature had won out, rather than the human spirit. The same mortal species that had the skill to create palaces, towers, bridges, churches and libraries, and the soul to make monumental works of art in music, painting and literature, apparently sought the steady destruction. In the years since, there has been no shortage of ammunition or weapons of war in the world, nor of the billionaires who supply them. Clear sighted as ever, Carnegie anticipated this and it gave him real pain. Like Burns, his lifelong mentor, he left a very different legacy.

Let's hope that another Burns or another Carnegie will appear. Better still, an embodiment of the two – the spirit and optimism of the former, the energy and enterprise of the latter, deeply rooted in love for their fellow creatures. Their spirit continues to speak to us in what Burns called 'the language of the soul'. A man might be a man, for a' that, but he can still be a brother to his fellow mortals.

John Cairney

Genius Illustrated from Burns

Andrew Carnegie

Reprinted from *Liber Scriptorum*, the first book of the Authors' Club, 1893

Days come to all in this life when control of the mind is lost. The brain refuses to be harnessed and to do our bidding. The will is no longer master. It refused to work or even to be interested. The charms pall which hitherto have never failed to allure it and bring it back to peace; but as these days of trial gradually soften, and hope returns, the unruly steed, the brain, submits again to some degree of discipline.

It was my fate last winter to pass through weary a month of agonising fear, and it may be interesting, perhaps, to others to note my experience, and learn what first enabled me to regain desired control of myself, for a man should no more permit his thoughts than his horse to run away with him. The brain must be made to tread the desired paths and answer bridle and spur instantly. He who cannot dismiss a subject from his thoughts at will is not master of himself. After many day and night walks around the library and the handling of book after book, every one more insipid than another, and all pushed back, and no rest found, it came upon me one day that a search through my favourite Burns for nothing but pure gems would be an interesting excursion. I should dig from the mine only gems, and build an Aladdin's palace of dazzling beauty with the glittering stones; should gather them together in a pile and gloat over them as the Prince of India over his jewels or the miser over his heaps of gold; should string them together as a rosary, and count by beads as holy men do, and thus bring peace to the troubled soul. No dainty repast upon the delicacies bred in a book would answer. I here must revel and gorge to surfeit – no sip of the nectar of the gods, but unlimited draughts, even to mental intoxication, would give peace and refuge from the 'brain still beating on itself'.

This ideal was the first which interested me. It naturally led to speculations upon the nature of literary genius.

Men have exercised themselves inventing definitions for genius, as men have sought for the Philosopher's Stone or for perpetual motion and with like disappointment, for none of these three things is to be found. Certainly, genius is not to be defined; it is a thing of the spirit, and assumes too many forms for words to embrace. 'An infinite capacity for taking trouble' is one attempt; 'genius is work', another. Both seemingly describe the very reverse of the quality to which we apply the word genius. 'Talent does what it can, genius what it must' comes nearer to it; true in a sense, but not all the truth. While it is impossible to define genius, I said to myself, let us try whether we cannot at least discern it, lay our fingers upon it, saying, Lo! Here is the genuine essence.

Gems are proverbially small. In the vast mines to literature we find them surrounded with much ordinary material. The gem itself is comprised in a line or a word, which should be easily recognised. When it is found we cry 'Eureka!' with safety. Here it is. This is genius. We say of much that precedes and follows this one line, or two, in rare instances this one word, or two: 'Several could have written this – talent is equal to it; but this one word, or line, never. That comes not from a talent below looking upward. The gods threw this from above and into the soul of genius.' Talent has climbed Parnassus, crag over crag, with us upon its shoulders, and called upon us to look back and enjoy the lovely pastoral scene below. Genius alone has scaled the height, and revealed to us the enchanted land beyond and over the mountain-top and all around the vaulted dome.

The 'fire' of genius, we say, and all are agreed that one essential element of genius is this 'fire'. No amount of smoke, no amount of heat suffices. The smoke passes away, the heat becomes intense, at the flame bursts forth, or genius there is none. Wherever genius touches, the divine spark sets fire to the pile.

The test of genius in any writer, therefore seems to be whether he has power to lead an understanding and sympathetic reader step by step, line after line, into regions more and more elevated, stirring the heart, the altar upon which the Godlike is placing the elements which he is set blazing anon.

It will be admitted that if the title of genius can be properly applied to any human being, it is to that phenomenon, the Scottish ploughman. No one questions but that he was a pure child of genius.

I took the works of the poet from their place of honour, next those of the 'god of gods' in the kingdom of poetry. My working copy begins with the 'Twa Dugs', the Newfoundland of the lordling, with its 'braw brass collar', and the other, the wisest and truest

of all, that which creeps farthest into the core of the heart – the
Scotch collie. The dog of the poor poet describes the joys of his
own humble home. Here is a picture of the home of honest poverty
which sets all dancing, young and old, as happy as only careless
poverty can be:

> *As bleak-fac'd Hallowmas returns,*
> *They get the jovial, ranting kirns,*
> *When rural life, o' ev'ry station,*
> *Unite in common recreation;*
> *Love blinks, Wit slaps, an' social Mirth*
> *Forgets there's Care upo' the earth.*
> *...*
>
> *The canty auld folks crackin' crouse,*
> *The young anes rantin' thro' the house –*
> *My heart has been sae fain to see them,*
> *That I for joy hae barkit wi' them.*

Here in one line lies the gem; here is genius. The elements have
taken fire. That collie has a soul; he is one of the family, as the
collie always is in the home of the Scotch peasant. Every collie in
the world has been elevated in social status since the pen of genius
made him one of that joyous throng. He sings his song, speaks his
piece, dances with the rest, and contributes his part to the general
happiness. Talent would probably have forgotten him altogether. It
could never have seen that the needed music to cap the joyous scene
might be invoked out of his bark. No; that is just the one step, the
'little more' of Michel Angelo's definition of genius.

Two lines at the close of this poem call for notice. These hairy philosophers sitting on the heather hills have told each other much of the trials and disadvantages of life in the palace and in the cottage; for there are advantages and disadvantages in both, though we have Marcus Aurelius' word for it, that life can be lived well 'even in a palace'. The sun had set, the gloaming was coming on –

> *When up they gat, and shook their lugs,*
> *Rejoic'd they werena men but dugs.*

There is no use in enlarging upon that last line. The reader who does not feel it to be a stroke of genius can never be made to see it. But who can fail to feel it? The poem ends with it, and goes out in a blaze. The line crystallises and passes into literature as one of its gems. Genius, nothing but genius.

Burns, like Milton, always betrays an extraordinary partiality for the devil. It would be difficult to illustrate genius better than by quoting several lines from his address to that wicked imp. One is tempted to quote several, but let us take the last verse only:

> *But, fare you weel, auld Nickie-ben!*
> *O wad ye tak a thought an' men'!*
> *Ye aiblins might – I dinna ken –*
> *Still hae a stake –*
> *I'm wae to think upo' yon den,*
> *E'en for your sake!*

Talent, even of the highest order, would have stopped much short of such a farewell. It might have tendered some good advice, ponderously delivered. Genius alone could have suggested the possible repentance and reformation of the very spirit of evil; and the suggestion is so delicately conveyed – nothing of the preacher, no denunciation, just a friendly word at parting. And so Burns takes leave of his Infernal Majesty lovingly, anxious for his future improvement and happiness. The poet would not do even Old Nick a bad turn; he would do him a good turn if he could. The spark is in this line. The glow of sympathy becomes all-pervading, sympathy with misfortune in all its phases, and we fell that he 'prayeth best who' not only 'loveth best all things, both great and small.' but all things, even evil things, loveth he so, that he prays their return to the better path.

The dying words of poor Mailie, the ploughman's pet ewe, furnish several gems. The dying sheep gives advice to her lambs and two lines inculcate a lesson at least as valuable as any other that can be given to lambs in the form of young men and women. For those who eschew bad company are:

> *But aye keep mind to moop an'mell*
> *We sheep o' credit like thysell.*

The address closes with the four following lines:

> *And now, my bairns, wi' my last breath,*
> *I lea'e my blessin' wi' you baith:*
> *An' when you think upo' your mither,*
> *Mind to be kin' to one another.*

A sermon in two lines for every family in the world. If there be brothers and sisters at variance anywhere who can withstand these lines and remain apart, Heaven help them! Not the note, this, which sets fire to the blood? But genius has another test not less searching than that of fire. The tear is also her own. The gracious drops from the fount of sorrow fall at her call. She alone strikes the hard heart with enchanted spear, and softens all into the sacred rain of tears.

In the 'Epistle to a Young Friend', amidst much good advice, we come to a stanza that blazes in these days of higher criticism and patching of human creeds which have too long passed for divine:

> *The fear o' Hell's a hangman's whip*
> *To hand the wretch in order;*
> *But where ye feel your honor grip,*
> *Let that aye be your border:*
> *Its slightest touches, instant pause –*
> *Debar a' side pretences;*
> *And resolutely keep its laws,*
> *Uncaring consequences.*

This sentiment will meet with general acceptance today. That Burns dared write it in his day is explicable only by the law that genius does what it must.

Matthew Arnold says that for dramatic force equal to that displayed in 'Tam o' Shanter' and 'The Jolly Beggars' we must look in the pages of Shakespeare alone. The scene in Alloway Kirk, with witches and warlocks in a dance, would obviously have been incomplete without the pretence of the head spirit of the fraternity himself. But what part would Old Nick play in such an entertainment? To dance with the others would scarcely have comported with his regal dignity: to stand apart would never do, for if there be any mischief afoot, he certainly must be in it. Goethe

makes Mephistopheles draw the wine from the cask and put the
sulphurous flame in it – a proper-part, no doubt: but these spirits
of the air neither eat nor drink, yet the devil must do something
among them. Here is the stroke of genius:

> *A winnock-bunker in the east,*
> *There sat Auld Nick, in shape o' beast;*
> *A towzie tyke, black, grim, an' large,*
> *To gie them music was his charge;*
> *He screw'd the pipes and gart them skirl,*
> *Till root and rafters a' did dirl.*

He gets at the very core of the whole matter. Without music no
dance was possible, and Nanie could never have 'lapped and flang'.
Those who dance must pay the piper; and when Auld Nick himself
sets the tune, as he often does, the devil's to pay indeed; his scale of
charges known no maximum, and he is a sure collector. The next
lines have a weird touch which is hand indeed to equal. One line
contains the searched-for spark:

> *Coffins stood round, like open presses,*
> *That shaw'd the dead in the last dresses;*
> *And by some dev'lish cantraip slight*
> *Each in its cauld hand held a light…*

The idea of ranging the dead in their coffins around the ballroom of
these spirits of darkness in their orgy might possibly have occurred
to a clever poet; but what of the last touch? The 'little more' lies
just here – the cold hands of corpses made to serve as candlesticks
to light the revels: the element of the awful is thus introduced with

appalling power. What a background for the picture! Mirth and revelry – life at its flood; the living ringed in and lighted up by the dead!

'Tam o' Shanter' has too many of the sparks to be quoted fully – the picture of Tam's home at the farm, for instance, when he was revelling at night in Ayr:

> *Whare sits our sulky, sullen dame,*
> *Gath'rin her brows like gath'rin storm,*
> *Nursin' her wrath to keep it warm.*

The finger goes at once upon the last line. Burns knew the sex. Most wives are too good, sweet, tender, and self-sacrificing to do more than make-believe when they rebuke. Their wrath needs constant fuel, or down it all goes, perhaps too soon.

In all that Burns has written there is nothing finer than 'The Vision'. He paints himself sitting in his hovel at night, the very den of poverty – an 'auld clay biggin' filled with tormenting smoke. At last he falls asleep, and the 'Genius of Scotland' comes to him in a dream. From beginning to end this is a poem filled with brightest gems, rich in the divine sparks of genius. Mark the description of Scotia's Guardian Angel, who presides over the inspired natures who have made that little land one of the largest domains in the realm of the spirit, and the home of Poetry, Romance, and Song.

'The Vision' tells him to 'preserve the dignity of man with soul erect', and then follows the close. The highest test of the poet is the manner in which he touches the supernatural.

Men may easily call spirits from the vasty deep, but how to use them so that we preserve our gravity is known to few. Very few men, it is said, know how to take their departure from a room becomingly. It has troubled many a writer how to dispose of his supernatural visitor, and prevent 'exit ghost' being followed by peals of laughter. What genius can do is seen in Hamlet's 'Remember me' as he noiselessly glides away. Banquo's exit with finger pointing to bloody throat is magnificent. True sparks indeed, especially the latter; but even with that may we not rank this departure of 'The Vision '?

> *'And wear thou this,' – she solemn said,*
> *And bound the holly round my head:*
> *The polished leaves, and berries red,*
> *Did rustling play;*
> *And, like a passing thought, she fled*
> *In light away.*

How could that peasant ploughman in his smoky den ever conceive anything so exquisitely delicate as this ending! I know nothing of the kind so perfect. One fondly lingers over –

> *And, like a passing thought, she fled*
> *In light away.*

Two words, but a Koh-i-noor. Genius! Inspiration!

There is something splendid in this poor ploughman greeting himself, as a matter of course, as the inspired bard and placing the holly upon his own royal head. Supreme genius does know its powers and its heritage. Burns was indeed the Bard of Scotland and the rightful king. No man has risen to dispute his title to the crown. The holly still remains there, its leaves greener and its berries redder to-day than when bound around his head.

The address to a mouse has been often quoted, but not the lines which to me contain the purest spark. Take the second stanza:

> *I'm truly sorry Man's dominion*
> *Has broken Nature's social union,*
> *An' justifies that ill opinion*
> *Which makes thee startle*
> *At me, thy poor, earth-born companion,*
> *An' fellow-mortal!*

Here is Darwinism for you. Talent could never have reached down so far as to become 'fellow-mortal' to a mouse. Or if it might have condescendingly done this much, it never could have elevated the poor little mouse to companionship with man. It took genius to divine and so to announce in this fashion that 'all flesh is kin'.

Here is an epitaph upon his friend and benefactor, Gavin Hamilton, from whom President Arthur was proud to claim descent. I remember he corrected me one day when I spoke of Gavin Hamilton. 'Not Gavin Hamilton,' said he. 'You ought to know better. He was one of my ancestors, and it was always Gaunin with my grandfather.'

> *The poor man weeps – here Gavin sleeps,*
> *Whom canting wretches blam'd:*
> *But with such as he – where'er he be,*
> *May I be sav'd or damn'd!*

We all know those in this world with whom we should be willing to take our chances in the next, now that Burns has put the idea into our heads; but who else would have gone so far as to print it for the first time?

We have not yet touched upon his songs. Take Bruce's Address, which Carlyle has called 'The war-hymn of the ages'. 'The first stanza of "Scots wha hae",' said mediocrity – in the person of Thompson, the publisher – 'will never do; no leader would dare offer as an alternative to victory a gory bed to troops he wished to encourage.' Death has been hailed, but death seems vague in comparison, and carries with it the suggestion of immediate passage to the abode of heroes. But Burns knew better than his critic, and replied: 'That line must stand.' And it stands for all time.

> *Welcome to your gory bed*
> *Or to victory.*

'Scotland's right' or the 'gory bed', the last welcome if the first fell. He stood for Scotland, body and soul, future or no future, Walhallas or Annihilation – it mattered not. At that supreme moment it was 'Scotland forever!'

In the well-known song, 'John Anderson, my jo', we have the spark. Has any poet ever given in one verse such a picture of the union of two hearts as this?

> *Now we maun totter down, John,*
> *But And hand in hand we'll go,*
> *...*
> *And sleep thegither at the foot,*
> *John Anderson, my jo.*

Up the hill, down the hill, through life, through death; 'until death us do part' is the vow of marriage; but when true marriage comes, death itself forces no separation. Through the dark shadow hand in hand – and this much for comfort and content – we shall 'sleep thegither at the foot', certain as we lie down that there can be no heaven for one without the other, and prepared for anything in the future, so we share it together.

'To Mary in Heaven' seems not only so perfect, but so sacred that one instinctively hesitates to quote from it. It is the ideal of lover's lament as clearly as 'Scots wha hae' is the war song, or 'Auld Lang Syne' the song of good fellowship, or 'A man's a man for a' that' the song of democracy. But four lines I must quote, which follow the description of the meeting on the banks of Ayr, which, 'gurgling, kissed this pebbled shore':

> *Still o'er these scenes my mem'ry wakes,*
> *And fondly broods with miser care!*
> *Time but the impression stronger makes,*
> *As streams their channels deeper wear.*

What Burns might have been had Mary lived to be his wife opens the field of boundless conjecture. The history of this incomparable lament is fittingly touching. His wife tells that, the poet not coming in at the usual evening hour, she in search of him and found him lying on his back on a hayrick gazing at the Evening Star, so absorbed that she did not disturb him. He came in later, and going to his table, took pen and wrote this lament.

The rapid change of mood in Burns has given rise to much surprise. Scott's devotion to his first love, whose sacred name he was discovered carving in Runic characters when he was an old man, tells the tale in his case. This is contrasted with the succession of favourites of Burns; but he too, though he sighed to many, loved but one. How sorry one is for the woman who was his wife: in the heart of her husband another sits enthroned. And what a line is that first one of the lament – six words of exquisite beauty, and such rhythm, shedding around the kindly light of genius:

> *Thou ling'ring star, with less'ning ray,*
> *That lov'st to greet the early morn,*
> *Again thou usher'st in the day*
> *My Mary from my soul was torn.*

Truly, 'Who says he has loved has never loved at all.'

And here comes 'Holy Willie's Prayer'. But this is no spark, the torch of genius illuminates every verse. We cannot pass it over altogether, and we might as well take the first stanza as any other:

> *O Thou, that in the heavens does dwell!*
> *Wha, as it pleases best Thysel!*
> *Sends ane to heaven, and ten to hell,*
> *A' for Thy glory,*
> *And no' for ony guid or ill*
> *They've done afore thee!*

In 'The Twa Herds' there is the spark –

> *Then Orthodoxy yet may prance,*
> *An' Learning in a woody dance,*
> *An' that fell cur ca'd Common Sense,*
> *That bites sae sair,*
> *Be banished o'er the sea to France:*
> *Let him bark there.*

Common sense does bite, indeed!

Matthew Arnold declares 'The Jolly Beggars' the greatest work of Burns. Shakespeare alone, says he, equalled it for dramatic force. It is the veteran's turn to amuse the old tatterdemalions, and he gives them a rollicking song indeed.

> *I lastly was with Curtis among the floating batt'ries,*
> *And there I left for witness an arm and a limb,*
> *Yet let my country need me, with Elliot to head me,*
> *I'd clatter on my stumps at the sound of a drum.*

The one line again. If there be in literature such a picture as that suggested by the last line, I have not met with it. Did Burns painfully think that out? Muse over it? Labour away at that part or this part of it? Or did the idea flash upon him like a stroke of lightning, and reveal that veteran moved to dancing upon his stumps at the very sound of the drum. I believe it burst upon the poet at once, and that he was afraid he might lose the flash before he could write it down. But we must pass to the closing song which is sung as an encore by the bard of the gang, after which the curtain falls. The first and last verses I quote:

See! The smoking bowl before us.
Mark our jovial, ragged ring!
Round and round take up the chorus,
And in raptures let us sing.

Chorus

A fig for those by law protected!
Liberty's a glorious feast!
Courts for cowards were erected,
Churches built to please the priest.
...

Life is all a variorum,
We regard not how it goes:
Let them cant about decorum
Who have characters to lose.

Here's to budgets, bags and wallets
Here's to all the wandering train!
Here's our ragged brats and callets!
One and all cry out – Amen!

There is an amen chorus for you! The most gloriously wild rant in literature, as far as I know, is this cantata. No wonder it was not published until after the death of the poet. If any many ever lived but Burns who could have written it, I have never heard of him. If he had never written anything else but this, he could never have been ignored as a poet.

In the next we strike my favourite of all songs. I confess that with songs and tunes I am as fickle as Burns was with his favourite lassies; one queen gives place to another with surprising facility. Every summer spent on the moors among the heather brings a new favourite. But there also comes a loyal return to a former love now and then; one that has reigned before and been dethroned for a time is restored and reigns again. Though not hereditary monarchs, these queens are eligible for re-election. Thus, 'My Nanie's Awa' has served more terms than any, and is now again in the high office of Queen of Song. It is a shame to quote any part of it, because every line seems a necessary step leading higher and higher until the region of fire is entered; but two verses must be singled out from this prime favourite of the hour, as the highest crests where all is mountainous.

> *The snaw-droop and primrose our woodlands adorn,*
> *And violets bathes in the weet o' the morn;*
> *They pain my sad bosom, sae sweetly they blaw,*
> *Thy mind me o' Nanie – and Nanie's awa'!*

> *Thou lav'rock that springs fae the dews of the lawn,*
> *The shepherd to warn o' the grey-breaking dawn,*
> *And thou, mellow mavis, that hails the night- fa',*
> *Give over for pity – my Nanie's awa'!*

Lying open before me on the opposite page comes the hymn of Triumphant Democracy:

> *The rank is but the guinea's stamp,*
> *The man's the gowd for a' that!*

The last verse sends that hymn singing throughout the world –

Then let us pray that come it may –
As come it may for a' that –
That sense and worth, o'er a' the earth,
May bear the gree, and a' that.

For a' that, and a' that,
It's comin' yet for a' that,
That man to man, the world o'er,
Shall brithers be for a' that!

This was before Tennyson sang of the Parliament of Man and the Federation of the World. Burns, with the true insight of the Poet-Prophet, proclaims the brotherhood of man.

I cannot leave my favourite in an attitude more pleasing than singing the brotherhood of man.

Whether these pages ever see the light or no, they have served their purpose, for many a weary anxious hour has the search for gems saved the writer, bringing to something like calm, and once more 'the taste of elevated joys', which comes to the tranquil mind.

Address by Andrew Carnegie at the unveiling of a statue to Burns, erected by the citizens of Montrose 1912

Provost and fellow citizens of Montrose, we are met today to testify that the immortal Bard still lives in our memory, that his fame increases with time – that his place in the world as in our hearts strengthens with the years – and that the debt we owe him is indeed unpayable. No man who ever lived has so many memorial statues in so many lands, and yet we meet today in Montrose to dedicate still another. It was not his genius, his insight, his vision, his wit or spirit of manly independence, nor all of these combined, which captured the hearts of men. It was his spontaneous, tender, all-pervading sympathy with every form of misfortune, pain or grief; not only in man but in every created form of being. He loved all living things, both great and small. Repeated are the proofs of this overflowing tenderness. The nest of the mouse destroyed by the plough which had 'cost many a weary nibble' appeals to his heart and the lesson is enforced:

> But mousie thou art no thy lane,
> In proving foresight may be vain;
> The best laid schemes o' mice an' men
> Gang aft agley
> An' lea'e us nought but grief an' pain
> For promised joy.

Burns seems to have divined what science today proclaims, that all
life is kin – listen to this outburst of emotion:

I'm truly sorry man's dominion
Has broken Nature's social union
An' justifies that ill opinion
Which makes thee startle
At me, thy poor earth-born companion
An' fellow mortal.

We murmur to ourselves, 'beyond this it is impossible for mortal to
go, this must be the utmost limit', but wait a moment, we are told
that talent does what it can but genius what it must, and Burns,
sweeping upward and onward under this Law startled the world
by his next leap, clear out of all bounds, at which it still keeps
wondering, for no mortal before or since has ever dared to entertain
the idea of reformation and pardon for the Evil One.

But fare-you-weel, auld 'Nickle-ben'
O wad ye tak a thought an' men'.
Ye aiblins micht – I dinna ken –
Still hae a stake
I'm wae to think upo' yon den,
Ev'n for your sake.

The poet was ever the reformer, and true to his mission he
ventures to intimate that his Infernal Majesty might vary one of his
recreations with advantage:

I'm sure sma' pleasure it can gie,
E'en to a deil,
To skelp and scaud poor dogs like me
An' hear us squeal.

In such familiar terms Burns addresses the Arch Fiend, enemy of
God and man – whom Milton thus describes:

Incensed with indignation, Satan stood
Unterrified, and like a comet burned

...

In the Arctic sky, and from his horrid hair
Shakes pestilence and war.

Fortunately, the stern doctrines literally interpreted in the poet's
day remain with us in our day only as helpful allegories in man's
progress to higher conceptions. Not till another poet reaches this
towering height upon which today one sits alone in solitude can
the ascendancy of Burns ever be questioned as the genius of the
overflowing, sympathetic heart, ever alive to the sorrows of man,
beast, mouse or devil.

There are two stanzas which give Burns high place as a truly
religious teacher of men:

The fear o' Hell's a hangman's whip.
To haud the wretch in order,
But where you find your honour grip,
Let that aye be your border,
Its slightest touches, instant pause

Debar a' side pretences;
And resolutely keep its laws,
Uncaring consequences.

In 'The Cotter's Saturday Night' we have the finest picture of
humble life ever painted, inculcating the most truly religious lesson:

Compar'd with this, how poor Religion's pride.
In all the pomp of method, and of art;
When men display to congregations wide
Devotion's every grace, except the heart!
The Pow'r, incens'd, the pageant will desert.
The pompous strain, the sacerdotal stole;
But haply, in some cottage far apart,
May hear, well-pleas'd, the language of the soul;
And in his Book of Life the inmates poor enrol.

I venture to submit that one line of Burns has not received due
attention as constituting a rule of life – a pure gem: 'Thine own
reproach alone do fear.'

Having from our own conscience – the Judge within – received a
verdict of approval, we have little to fear from any other tribunal.
The 'Judge within' sits in the Supreme Court.

The prophets in days past were stoned, as Burns was, but the
assailants of Burns in his day were wrong. He saw the great
light before they did, as the prophets and leaders of mankind
invariably do and must do, else they were not prophets. The day
has now arrived when he, the proclaimer of the royalty of man,

stands revealed to us as the true Poet-Prophet of his age. What he proclaimed has proved to be the needed gospel for the advancement of man, especially for us of the English-speaking race.

I have ventured to hail him as the Poet-Prophet of his age. That he was a Poet will pass unquestioned, but was he not also a Prophet; did he not see in advance of his fellows the certain growth of the rights of man through the spread of democracy, and was he not awake to the crude and repulsive theology of his day, and at the same time saw the coming of the better day in which we now live, when the God of wrath who condemned man to everlasting torment has become displaced by the Heavenly Father, who can be trusted to deal mercifully even with the sinner? In these changes we recognise the work of Burns, it was he who laid the axe to the root of the tree of ignorance and superstition, and in doing so made mankind his debtor. Our Republic was founded upon the Rights of Man – his political gospel – which permeated both Britain and America – and in more recent times has won sway over all your self-governing colonies, Canada, Australia, and New Zealand, so that today Burns' political gospel rules our English-speaking race, which is marching steadily, though more slowly than we could wish, to the full fruition of the ideal of our Poet-Prophet.

Let us rejoice that we live in this age when the march of man upward is so pronounced. In one department the motherland is in advance of the republic and her colonies. She has established a law first proclaimed by another famous Scot, foremost of all in his branch of study. Adam Smith's *Wealth of Nations* marked an era in the world's history, and no statement made by him has proved so important for man's advance to true democracy as this:

> The subjects of every state ought to contribute towards
> the support of the government, as nearly as possible in
> proportion to their respective abilities; that is, in pro-
> portion to the revenue which they respectively enjoy
> under the protection of the State. In the observation or
> neglect of this maxim consists, what is called the equal-
> ity or inequality of taxation.

This doctrine was such a shock to the statesmen of the day that
even his editor, Professor Thorold Rogers, absorbed a full page in
small type to point out how his author had stumbled. In the view
of today, the injustice lies in not taxing according to value. This
just taxation the millionaires of the republic and colonies have so
far escaped, but their day is coming; and properly so. Let us rejoice
that the old home is here in the lead, an example for her children
to follow.

In *The Gospel of Wealth*, published here 20-odd years ago,
the graduated tax is advocated, and it is held that the modern
millionaires should receive part of the treatment proposed for
Shylock, under which, according to the laws of Venice, one-half of
his goods would 'come to the privy coffer of the state'. So should
it be with the hoards of the millionaires of our day, and this, not as
a punishment but for their own good, because it is just, and justice
alone insures general contentment.

On the other hand, while the motherland leads in just graduated
taxation, she is today following the younger branches of her race
in widening her franchise and establishing equal electoral districts,
and, above all, giving each man only one vote, thus making
all citizens equal. So the beneficent exchange goes on between

motherland and childlands – the parts of the vast empire of our
race ever drawing closer together, each contributing of its best to
the others in fair exchange, keeping our race ever in advance in
establishing the rights of man and marching steadily to perfection
when one citizen's privilege in the state becomes every citizen's
right as is the law in all the younger lands. Our race is thus
rapidly becoming a veritable brotherhood which may finally be
again united. The Bible in its marvellous translation, along with
Shakespeare and Burns, form the chief cementing bonds next to our
common language and common law.

The latest and most telling tribute paid Burns is that of your late
Member of Parliament, Lord Morley – and proud was he to be the
successor of Joseph Hume, and Member for what, in his opinion,
was the most intelligent constituency in the land. He told the
assembled editors of the empire, in effect, that a few lines
from Burns had done more to form and maintain the present
improved political and social conditions of the people than all the
millions of editorials ever written. I asked him to name the lines
he referred to, but he replied there was no need to name these to
me. Since I promised to be with you today, however, I have tried to
imagine what lines he had in mind. Here is probably the list, as I
should guess:

First:

> *While we sing God Save the King*
> *We'll ne'er forget the people.*

Second:

> *The rank is but the guinea-stamp.*
> *The man's the gowd for a' that.*

Third:

> *Man's true, genuine estimate,*
> *The grand criterion of his fate,*
> *Is not, art thou high or low?*
> *Did thy fortune ebb or flow?*
> *Wert thou cottager or king,*
> *Peer or peasant? No such thing.*

Fourth:

> *Ye see yon birkie ca'd a lord,*
> *Wha struts and stares an' a' that,*
> *Tho' hundreds worship at his word*
> *He's but a coof for a' that.*
> *For a' that and a' that,*
> *His riband, star, an' a' that.*
> *The man o' independent mind*
> *He looks and laughs at a' that.*

Fifth:

A prince can mak a belted knight,
A marquis, duke and a' that.
But an honest man's aboon his might,
Guid faith, he mauna fa' that.

Sixth:

Columbia's offspring, brave and free,
In danger's hour Still flaming in the van,
Ye know and dare proclaim the royalty of man.

These few lines from Burns are ample, and constitute the best platform ever formed to guard the wise and peaceful march of progress. No violence, no physical force, all peacefully and in order. Ballots, not bullets; argument, not riot; all classes hand-in-hand co-operating as members of one family for the general weal of all law-abiding classes ensures the happiness of every proper class.

And now may I be permitted to transport myself from my native to my adopted land for a few minutes. You well know that no part of the world has Burns more completely captured than the republic, now the home of the great majority of English-speaking people. It is not less conscious of all it owes to Burns than the motherland itself. But what can one say of the immortal bard which has not been better said already by his fellow poets and our literary masters? I shall select a few of their gems and let these tell their story.

It was said of Lincoln's republicanism that it was 'of the same spirit as the Gospel of his favourite, Burns'. As a lad at school he fortunately had a Scotch school master who adored Burns. The boy was carried away by the Bard, and it is recorded that when still a youth, wagers were made that no one could call upon him for a recitation from Burns which he could not give from memory. In his mature years, he lectured on his favourite poet, and as usual drew the masses of the people. Unfortunately, no trace of this lecture can now be found. We have searched for it in vain. What would one not give for a copy? Imagine Lincoln and Burns together, both 'men who held their patents of nobility direct from the hand of Almighty God'.

We have, however, a tribute to Burns from Lincoln's bosom companion and fellow orator, who divided the crowds with Lincoln in the anti-slavery campaign – Colonel Ingersoll – the most powerful, popular orator I have ever heard. Like Lincoln, he worshipped Burns, and kept upon his library table two beautifully bound volumes, one Shakespeare and the other Burns, which he called his Bible and his Hymn Book. He made a pilgrimage to the birthplace of Burns and wrote the following lines in the famous cottage:

> *Though Scotland boasts a thousand names*
> *Of patriot, king, and peer.*
> *The noblest, grandest of them all*
> *Was loved and cradled here.*
> *Here lived the gentle, peasant prince,*
> *The loving cotter-king,*
> *Compared with whom the greatest Lord*
> *Is but a titled thing.*

'Tis but a cot roofed in with straw,
A hovel made of clay;
One door shuts out the snow and storm,
One window greets the day.
And yet I stand within this room
And hold all thrones in scorn;
For here, beneath this lowly thatch,
Love's sweetest bard was born.

President Garfield realised that: 'rising above the trammels of birth and poverty, Burns spoke to the great nameless class of labouring men throughout the world while kings and nations listened in amazement. In the highest class of lyric poetry three names stand, their fame covers 18 centuries – one of these is Burns.'

Secretary of State Blaine says: 'Genius is not confined to lands or latitudes, Burns belonged to the world.'

Emerson declared that: 'Neither Latimer nor Luther struck such telling blows against false Theology as did this brave singer. The Declaration of Independence and the *Marseillaise* are not weightier documents in the history of freedom than the songs of Burns.'

Whittier tells us that: 'Burns lived on with a vitality which gathers strength from time. His fame broadens and deepens every year. The world has never known a truer singer.'

Bryant tells us the truth when he declares: 'Burns was great because God breathed into him in greater measure than any other man the spirit of that love which constitutes his own essence and made him more than any other man a living soul. Burns was great by the greatness of his sympathies.'

Hawthorne, at Burns' birthplace, declares: 'in this humble nook of all places in the world. Providence was pleased to deposit the germ of the richest human life which mankind had then within its circumference.'

Wendell Holmes says: 'Burns should have passed years of his life in America, for these words of his, "A man's a man for a' that", show that the true American feeling belonged to him as much as if he had been born on Bunker Hill.' Quite true, but born near Bannockburn is quite as effective.

Longfellow sings:

> *But still the music of his song*
> *Rises o'er all, elate and strong,*
>
> *Its Master chords*
> *Manhood, Freedom, Brotherhood.*

Speaker of Congress Henderson, a born Scot, declares: 'Robert Burns was also a preacher to humanity, and if this old earth of ours had more such preachers in its pulpits it would be a better world.'

Senator Hoar tells us that: 'Burns brought to the world the best message ever brought since Bethlehem, and humanity the world over walks more erect for what he said and sung. Genius sings through the soul of Burns like the wind through an Aeolian harp.'

Governor Knott declares: 'Burns possessed as no other man ever did, the universal alchemy of genius which enabled him to bring to light the pure virgin gold in everything he touched.'

Margaret Fuller writes: 'Burns is full of the noble genuine democracy which seeks not to destroy royalty, but to make all men kings as he was himself in nature.'

Bayard Taylor avers that: 'The stranger in foreign land comes to love Scotland and her people because Burns loved them.'

Beecher declares that: 'Burns has taught men the thoughts of God in nature more than a great many pulpits have.'

But why continue further in this strain? While the Poet-Prophet's prophesy, the grandest of all, that man to man the world o'er shall brothers be and a' that is not yet fulfilled, I do not hesitate to proclaim my unshaken faith that it is coming yet 'for a' that'.

Meanwhile, let us rejoice that within the wide boundaries of our English speaking race peace is at last accomplished. The vast majority in every land, 'if Shakespeare's tongue be spoken there and songs of Burns be in the air', would rise in mutiny and compel their rulers to submit any difference between them to peaceful arbitration. So much for the reign of peace and the prophecy of Burns, to the fulfilment of which we are steadily marching.

Lord Morley tells us in his recent Manchester address that a few books in political literature rank as Acts not Books, because they compelled the adoption of the ideas advanced, and that two of these were found in the Declaration of American Independence and another in Paine's *Common Sense*, which he declares 'the most influential political piece ever composed'.

Burns has given the world several of these precious jewels which have already fulfilled their mission within our entire race.

The rank is but the guinea's stamp,
The man's the gowd for a' that

is one, and here is another, the grandest of all his prophecies –

Then let us pray that come it may,
As come it will for a' that,
That man to man, the world o'er,
Shall brothers be for a' that.

As far as our race is concerned, war between its parts is today unthinkable. In its worldwide scope it still remains a prophecy, but never can these lines fail to thrill and incite to action the hearts of men, until their mission is fully accomplished and they learn war no more – they are immortal and can die only in triumph.

It is the general opinion of the world's wisest and best that Burns stands alone. All eulogies are concentrated in two which I have kept for the close – one from the American poet, Walt Whitman; the other from Horace Greely, the republic's greatest journalist, and son of a Scotch mother. Whitman's verdict is that: 'he was the most flesh and blood chiel ever cast up upon the sands of time.'

Greely declares: 'Of all the men who ever lived Burns nestles closest to the bosom of humanity.'

Of no other man can this be said, here he has no rival.

I now proceed to unveil the statue which Montrose has erected in memory of the Immortal Bard, tenderly wrapping him as it were in the folds of this last unrivalled tribute, which passes today unchallenged, for it is indeed true that Burns of all men that ever lived 'nestles today closest to the bosom of humanity'. Citizens of Montrose, you honour yourselves in honouring the man who has proved himself the Poet-Prophet of his age.

Burns statue, Montrose *(Photograph by Nick Birse, source Wikimedia Commons)*

The Philanthropy of Andrew Carnegie

It was at the age of just 33 that Andrew Carnegie first had
the idea to devote much of his present and future wealth to
benevolent causes. At his death, he had given away approximately
$340,000,000. What follows is a summary of this work which
illustrates his key areas of interest: education, research, technology,
heroism and peace. Since his death in August 1919, Carnegie's
wealth, running into many tens of millions of dollars, continues
to fund the philanthropic work carried out today by 22 global
institutions.

1896   Carnegie Institute

A campus in Pittsburgh consisting of the Institute of Technology,
a museum, a Library School, a Fine Arts Department and a main
library with eight branch libraries across the city.

$28m given by the end of 1918.

1902   Carnegie Institute of Washington

Consisting of research departments of experimental evolution,
marine biology, historical research (1903), economics and
sociology, terrestrial magnetism, the Mount Wilson Observatory, a
geophysical laboratory, botanical research, a nutrition laboratory,
meridian astrometry, embryology and eugenics. This Carnegie
Institute was given to print books not otherwise affordable.

$16.5m given by the end of 1918.

1904   Carnegie Hero Fund

To be given in times of peace. The first fund was for USA, Canada & Newfoundland. The Hero Fund, created to 'enhance the psychological value to the human race of the quality of individual human sacrifice', recognised 19,333 heroic acts and gave 1,430 awards by the end of 1918 for pensions, disasters and special appropriations, education, home purchase and debt removal. Subsequent funds were set up in Great Britain, France, Germany, Norway, Sweden, Italy, Denmark, Belgium, the Netherlands and Switzerland.

$2.4m by the end of 1918.

1905   Carnegie Foundation for the Advancement of Teaching

Inspired by a line from Robert Burns, 'Nae man can tether time or tide'. Provision of pensions for teachers which Carnegie saw as the least rewarded profession. Set up in the USA, Canada and Newfoundland. Eligible institutions had to be non-sectarian and awards were based on rule not request or recommendation. Limited to associated institutions and for those with college/university qualifications who had 'grown old' in teaching. A reserve fund was provided by the Carnegie Corporation.

$29m (including $1m for teacher annuities) by the end of 1918.

1910   Carnegie Endowment for International Peace

Set up to study the causes of war and how to prevent them. To further the development of international law, to educate public

THE PHILANTHROPY OF ANDREW CARNEGIE

opinion, bring countries together, to seek peaceful methods of settlement, to better understand international rights and duties. The HQ was in Washington, opposite the White House.

$3.2m by the end of 1918.

1911   Carnegie Corporation of New York

Established to provide funds for the advancement and diffusion of knowledge and understanding in the USA by aiding technical schools, libraries and scientific research.

$49.8m from 1911 to the end of 1918.

In the United Kingdom:

1901   Carnegie Trust for the Universities of Scotland

$10m given by the end of 1918.

1903   Carnegie Dunfermline Trust

$3.75m 1918.

1916   Carnegie UK Trust

$10m given by the end of 1918.

Other notable beneficiaries of Andrew Carnegie's philanthropy:

The Hague Peace Palace (1913) – $1.5m.

Endowment for Institutes at Homestead, Braddock, Duquesne and Pittsburgh – $1m.

Pension Fund for Steelworkers – $4m.

Free public libraries, library buildings and endowments – $80m.

Church organs – $6.2m.

Substantial funds were also given to educational establishments for black Americans, such as the Tuskegee Institute.

'the man who dies thus rich dies disgraced.'

ANDREW CARNEGIE

Select Bibliography

CARNEGIE

Carnegie, Andrew, *My Own Story*, Holmes, 1984

Round the World, Scribner's, 1884

An American Four-in-Hand in Britain, Scribner's, 1883

Triumphant Democracy, Scribner's, 1888

The Gospel of Wealth, 1900

The Empire of Business, Harper & Brothers, 1903

James Watt, Doubleday, Page & Co., 1913

Problems of Today, Doubleday, Page & Co., 1908

Autobiography, Houghton Mifflin, 1920

Hendrick, Burton J, *The Life of Andrew Carnegie*, Doubleday, Doran and Co., 1932

Nasaw, David, *Andrew Carnegie*, Penguin, 2006

Wall, Joseph Frazier, *Andrew Carnegie*, OUP, 1970

BURNS

Cairney, John, *A Moment White*, Outram Press, 1986

The Man Who Played Robert Burns, Mainstream Publishing, 1987

On the Trail of Robert Burns, Luath Press, 1999

The Luath Burns Companion, Luath Press, 2001

Immortal Memories, Luath Press, 2003

Burnscripts, Luath Press, 2011

Colvin, Calum, and Wilson, Rab, *Burnsiana: Artworks and Poems Inspired by the Life and Legacy of Robert Burns*, Luath Press, 2013

Grimble, Ian,
Robert Burns, Hamlyn, 1974

Hall, Andy,
Touched by Robert Burns,
Birlinn, 2008

Hecht, Hans,
Robert Burns:The Man and his Works,
William Hodge, 1936

Henley, WE, and Henderson, TF
(eds), *The Poetry of Burns*,
Jack, 1896

Hunter, Colin M,
and Hunter, Douglas M, *Illustrated History of the Family, Friends and Contemporaries of Robert Burns*,
Privately Printed, 2008

Law, Donald A,
Robert Burns: A Study,
Routledge and Keegan, Paul, 1974

Mackay, James A,
Burns: A Biography,
Mainstream Publishing, 1990

Lindsay, Maurice (ed),
The Burns Encyclopaedia,
4th edition,
Robert Hale, 2013

Wallace, William (ed),
The Poetical Works of Robert Burns,
Chambers, 1958

Westwood, Peter J,
The Deltiology of Robert Burns,
Creedon Publications, 1994

More Information

carnegiebirthplace.com

carnegie.org

carnegiehero.org.uk

burnsmuseum.org.uk

rbwf.org.uk

The Andrew Carnegie Birthplace Museum is located in Moodie Street, Dunfermline, Fife KY12 7PL

The Robert Burns Birthplace Museum is located at Murdoch's Loan, Alloway, Ayr KA 4PQ

Luath Press Limited

committed to publishing well written books worth reading

LUATH PRESS takes its name from Robert Burns, whose little collie Luath *(Gael.,* swift or nimble) tripped up Jean Armour at a wedding and gave him the chance to speak to the woman who was to be his wife and the abiding love of his life. Burns called one of the 'Twa Dogs' Luath after Cuchullin's hunting dog in Ossian's *Fingal.* Luath Press was established in 1981 in the heart of Burns country, and is now based a few steps up the road from Burns' first lodgings on Edinburgh's Royal Mile.
Luath offers you distinctive writing with a hint of unexpected pleasures.

Most bookshops in the uk, the us, Canada, Australia, New Zealand and parts of Europe, either carry our books in stock or can order them for you. To order direct from us, please send a £sterling cheque, postal order, international money order or your credit card details (number, address of cardholder and expiry date) to us at the address below. Please add post and packing as follows: uk – £1.00 per delivery address; overseas surface mail – £2.50 per delivery address; overseas airmail – £3.50 for the first book to each delivery address, plus £1.00 for each additional book by airmail to the same address. If your order is a gift, we will happily enclose your card or message at no extra charge.

Luath Press Limited
543/2 Castlehill
The Royal Mile
Edinburgh EH1 2ND
Scotland
Telephone: +44 (0)131 225 4326 (24 hours)
Fax: +44 (0)131 225 4324
email: sales@luath. co.uk
Website: www. luath.co.uk